J.S. Bach's
Keyboard Technique:

A Historical Introduction

J.S. Bach's Keyboard Technique:

A Historical Introduction

Quentin Faulkner

Publishing House
St. Louis

Library of Congress Catalog Data

Faulkner, Quentin.
    J. S. Bach's keyboard technique.

    Bibliography: p.
    1. Bach, Johann Sebastian, 1685-1750. I. Title.

ML410.B1F38 1984   786.1 ′092 ′4   84-5866
ISBN 0-570-01326-7

1 2 3 4 5 6 7 8 9 10 MAL 93 92 91 90 89 88 87 86 85 84

BIOGRAPHICAL SKETCH OF QUENTIN FAULKNER

Quentin Faulkner is presently associate professor of organ and music theory/history at the University of Nebraska—Lincoln. His undergraduate work was at Westminster Choir College, Princeton, NJ, and his graduate study at Southern Methodist University, Dallas, TX, and Union Theological Seminary, New York City, from which he holds the degree of doctor of sacred music. He also holds the associate degree in the American Guild of Organists. Before coming to Nebraska in 1974, Mr. Faulkner served as the assistant organist at the Cathedral Church of St. John the Divine, New York City. In addition to teaching organ, he has developed a series of courses in church music at the UN-L School of Music.

Acknowledgments

It is almost unseemly that the author of a tiny book such as this one should be so deeply indebted to others, both for its form as well as its substance. I cannot but confess that this is so, and consequently record here my sincere gratitude to all the kind people to whom the virtues if any (though none of the faults) of this volume must in large measure be credited:

The University of Nebraska—Lincoln Research Council, which awarded me a Maude Hammond Fling Summer Fellowship in 1980 and subsequently a travel grant for research further afield; these awards enabled me to complete most of this book.

Susan Messerli, University of Nebraska-Lincoln music librarian, who spared no effort to obtain materials I needed, and who, together with her husband Carlos Messerli, read an early draft of this work.

My organ students, who have taught me more about Bach's keyboard technique than I have taught them.

Gene Bedient, organ builder, whose organs were a primary source of inestimable value in helping me understand the implications of my research and my conclusions.

Raymond Haggh, director of the UN-L School of Music, to whose wisdom, scholarship, and sense of proportion this book owes a large portion of whatever accuracy, balance, and fairness it possesses.

George Ritchie, UN-L professor of organ, colleague and friend, without whose advice and stimulation this book could not have happened.

The staffs of various libraries, both in the U.S. and abroad, especially Bill Parsons and the Library of Congress Music Division, whose prompt help sped this project along.

Harald Vogel, Norddeutsche Orgelakademie, to whom we are all indebted for the fundamental insights into early keyboard practices he has given us.

Howard M. Brown, University of Chicago; Gerald Frank, Oklahoma State University; Philip R. Frowery; William Porter, Oberlin Conservatory of Music; George Stauffer, Hunter College and Columbia University; Christoph Wolff, Harvard University; Jean-Claude Zehnder, Schola Cantorum Basiliensis, all of whom read the typescript and made valuable suggestions.

Ernest May, University of Massachusetts-Amherst, whose help and hospitality benefited this book in ways that will immediately be apparent to him.

George Klump, Loyola-Marymount University, under whose guidance I first became aware of earlier keyboard performance practices.

Eugenia Earle, Manhattan School of Music, whose exquisite performance and firm tutelage implanted in me an indelible awareness of "le bon gout."

Richard French, Yale University, whose eagle eye for things scholarly would never let me get away with anything (including errors in the typescript), and whose scholarly good sense formed whatever of that rare quality I possess.

Rodney Schrank, Concordia Publishing House, whose gracious "midwifery" smoothed the birth of this book.

Richard Larson, my neighbor, whose enthusiasm for my work spurred me on in my labors.

Mary Murrell Faulkner, organist and my wife, whose unfailing support and unparalleled understanding of the complexities of this undertaking make her very glad it is done.

Contents

Introduction

The purpose of this introduction to J. S. Bach's keyboard technique is threefold:

1. to present the extant evidence relating to Bach's keyboard technique

2. to use this evidence as a basis for conjecturing a comprehensive and unified picture of his technique

3. to reveal this technique as capable of equipping present-day keyboard performers to play the music of Bach with security and ease.

This project grew both out of scholarly curiosity and a desire to speak to the considerable interest in performance practices of early music that has continued to grow throughout the 20th century. Although it is founded on a thorough reexamination of primary sources, it is unavoidably indebted to earlier discourses on the matters it treats, beginning with the pioneering work of Arnold Dolmetsch, first published in the early part of this century.[1]

This study might equally well have been called "An Introduction to the Keyboard Technique of J. S. Bach's Students." Bach himself, from all reports, seems to have been one of those rare, extraordinarily gifted keyboard performers born with such superb technique and coordination that no technical difficulty presents much of a challenge to them. Bach's keyboard technique is perhaps inimitable. But what he taught his students—those of less exalted ability than his—is probably more valuable to us than what he himself was capable of doing at the keyboard.

The following pages seek to present, to analyze, and to evaluate the concrete evidence about technique and execution—the actual fingering patterns used, along with statements on keyboard technique and performance practices by Bach's sons and students. It is to this evidence (though admittedly preserved only fragmentarily) that this study will be confined, insofar as possible.

In Bach's time, as in ours, there were countless unwritten assumptions about musical performance; furthermore, musicians of the period (in particular unique talents such as J. S.

[1]Arnold Dolmetsch, *The Interpretation of Music of the Seventeenth and Eighteenth Centuries* (London: Novello, 1915; corrected edition, 1946), pp. 364 ff. Other scholars who have written on this subject include:

Babitz, Sol. "On Using Early Keyboard Fingering," *Diapason*, February, March, and April 1969.

Donington, Robert. *The Interpretation of Early Music.* London: Faber & Faber, [1963]. Pp. 410 f.; 514 f.

Ferguson, Howard. *Keyboard Interpretation.* New York & London: Oxford University Press, 1975. Pp. 53 f.; 67 f.

LeHuray, Peter. "On Using Early Keyboard Fingerings: A Sequel," *Diapason*, June, July, and August 1969.

Zehnder, Jean-Claude. "Organ Articulation in the Seventeenth and Eighteenth Centuries," *The American Organist*, Part I, Vol. 17, No. 7 (July 1983); Part II, Vol. 17, No. 12 (December 1983); revised reprint of "Zur Artikulation im Orgelspiel des 17. und 18. Jahrhunderts," *Musik und Gottesdienst*, Vols. 2 & 3, 1977.

———. "Alte Fingersätze," *Ars Organi*, September 1980, pp. 16 ff.

Bach) would have exhibited in their playing the same sort of subtle nuances that lend conviction to fine playing today.[2] Yet these must forever remain matters of conjecture, and therefore (while fascinating to consider) they are not mentioned here. The study is limited to matters about which, through musical and literary evidence, it is possible to ascertain enough to remove them to some extent from the realm of speculation. Any later interpretation (such as this one) inevitably manipulates and colors information; but the closer it remains to empirical evidence, the less fanciful will be the image it creates. Many things must continue to remain matters of conjecture, since musical performance is inextricably bound with the tastes and prejudices of its age—a limitation that is of course both frustrating and continually challenging.

There are two procedural preferences that underlie the research and composition of this essay. First, in dealing with the material at hand I have accorded primary attention and weight to those sources stemming directly from J.S. Bach and his students. There is a rather large amount of primary source material on keyboard performance from the late baroque period, and some of it is contradictory—the inevitable consequence of differences in taste among countries and among individual musicians. Sources outside Bach's immediate circle of influence (i. e., students and close associates) are valuable for our purposes only insofar as they corroborate and amplify ideas and techniques of those within the circle.[3] The following conclusions regarding Bach's keyboard technique are therefore based on the assumption that proximity to Bach coupled with consistency of ideas between sources insures reliability of information.

The second presupposition behind the work at hand determines the relative weight assigned to the evidence from the Bach circle. The majority (and certainly the most important) of Bach's keyboard works—the fugues, most of the preludes and chorale settings—are thoroughly polyphonic in texture. In performing them, each of the performer's hands must execute at least two independent musical lines at the same time. In addition, keyboard works (especially those for the organ) do not use scale passagework to a great degree; they are rather built up of small and curiously wrought motives. For both of these reasons, scale fingerings (as found in various 18th-century manuscripts and publications, including C. P. E. Bach's *Versuch über die wahre Art das Clavier zu spielen*) are less valuable in determining fingering practices and basic articulation than are the few polyphonic works with fingerings from Bach's circle that have been preserved. The latter have proved to be of decisive significance for the conclusions arrived at in this study.

---

[2]Early primary sources that discuss matters of style and taste in performance include: C. P. E. Bach, *Versuch über die wahre Art das Clavier zu spielen* (Berlin: C. F. Henning & G. L. Winter, 1753 & 1762); J. G. Leopold Mozart, *Versuch einer gründlichen Violinschule* (Augsburg: J. J. Lotter, 1756); and J. J. Quantz, *Versuch einer Anweisung die Flöte traversiere zu spielen* (Berlin: J. F. Voss, 1752). The information and opinions these sources offer, though frequently enlightening, often reflect the ideas and tastes of the generation following J. S. Bach and must therefore be applied to Bach's music with caution.

[3]It follows from this assumption that the preponderance of source material postdates J. S. Bach's life and thus inevitably reflects in some measure the ideas and tastes in musical performance of later generations. This is certainly the case, for example, with two of the major sources, C. P. E. Bach and J. N. Forkel; consequently some scholars have questioned the reliability of later sources such as these. Even a brief exposure to C. P. E. Bach's music certainly demonstrates how greatly his musical style differs from his father's; his book on keyboard performance likewise reflects this stylistic difference. With Forkel the case is even more problematic, since his information is all secondhand (albeit from reliable sources and conscientiously edited). Forkel's biography is colored by the occasional intrusion of his own rather romantic conception of Bach as the towering artistic genius. It is also a derivative source. Yet, we ask, in the more objective reporting on matters of *technique* what can we trust more? Surely not the ideas of Bach's contemporaries, most of whom never had anything to do with him. If we slight or dismiss the information on technique provided us by C. P. E. Bach and by Forkel (especially when all the relevant sources are in solid agreement about that information), what are we to substitute for it? Only our own opinions, which are likely to be far more speculative and arbitrary than their reports.

The Nature of the Evidence

A. PRIMARY SOURCE MATERIAL

1. The *Applicatio* (BWV 994), the first piece of music found in the *Clavier-büchlein vor Wilhelm Friedemann Bach* (dating from 1720— ; the manuscript is now in the library of the Yale University School of Music). It is preserved in Bach's handwriting (see facsimile, p. 25).

2. The *Praeambulum* (BWV 930), the ninth piece of music in the same volume; likewise in Bach's handwriting (see facsimile, p. 26).

No autograph source material is extant concerning any aspect of Bach's keyboard technique other than the fingering indications these two pieces bear. Without the decisive secondary source material described below, it would be difficult to construct any image of Bach as a keyboard player.

B. DECISIVE SECONDARY SOURCE MATERIAL

Because it stems from Bach's immediate circle, because it corroborates the autograph sources described above, and because there is (as this study aims to demonstrate) a high degree of internal consistency among its various components, the following secondary source material may be considered decisive in the formation of a more complete picture of Bach's keyboard technique:

1. Carl Philipp Emanuel Bach's *Versuch über die wahre Art das Clavier zu spielen* (Berlin: C. F. Henning & G. L. Winter, Part I, 1753), without doubt the most complete and helpful source; hereinafter referred to as *Versuch*. William J. Mitchell has translated it into English as *Essay on the True Art of Playing Keyboard Instruments* (New York: W. W. Norton, [1949]); hereinafter referred to as "Mitchell." This translation has been amended for accuracy and completeness where necessary.

2. *Prelude & Fugetta* (spelled thus in the manuscript) in C major, BWV 870a, an early version of the first prelude and fugue from the second part of *Das wohltemperierte Clavier* (see score, pp. 27—29). Until recently the manuscript containing BWV 870a was thought to be lost (it is printed in Volume 36 of the *Bach Gesellschaft Ausgabe*, pp. 224—25), but it has in fact come to light as BB Mus. ms. P1089, whose scribe Hans-Joachim Schulze has identified as Johann Caspar Vogler, Bach's student and successor at Weimar.[4] On the basis of the manuscript's watermarks, Schulze has established the date of the manuscript to be between 1727 and 1731 (Vogler was in Leipzig during December of 1729 as an—unsuc-

---

[4]Hans-Joachim Schulze, " 'Das Stück in Goldpapier': Ermittlungen zu einigen Bach-Abschriften des fréihen 18. Jahrhunderts" (*Bach-Jahrbuch*, 1978), pp. 19—42.

cessful—candidate for the post of organist at the Nicolaikirche).

3. Johann Philipp Kirnberger's *Clavierübungen mit der Bachischen Applicatur* (4 Sammlungen. Berlin: Friedrich Wilhelm Birnstiel, 1761, 1762, 1763, 1766), in particular the "Allabreve" on pp. 14 and 15 of the third *Sammlung* (see facsimile, p. 30). Kirnberger was a student of J. S. Bach (probably 1739—41) and a close associate of Emanuel Bach in Berlin.

4. Johann Nicolaus Forkel's *Über Johann Sebastian Bachs Leben, Kunst und Kunstwerke* (Leipzig, 1802), translated in the *Bach Reader*[5] (hereinafter referred to as "Forkel"). Forkel was Bach's first biographer. In preparing the volume he relied to a great extent on information given him by C. P. E. Bach and Wilhelm Friedemann Bach, J. S. Bach's two eldest and most gifted sons. Thus it was in preparation for many years before its publication (Friedemann Bach died in 1784, Emanuel in 1788). It has proved to be remarkably accurate and comprehensive; the section on Bach as a keyboard player is of inestimable value in gaining an understanding of Bach's keyboard technique.

5. Works from Bach's circle with indications of fingering. In addition to the fingering indications by Vogler and Kirnberger described above, there are numerous other manuscript sources that contain fingerings. These sources are listed in Appendix I. Unfortunately the manuscripts that bear extensive fingerings are from the hands of scribes who cannot be conclusively identified as direct students of J. S. Bach (this is the case in particular with J. G. Preller). On the other hand, those works that are unquestionably from the hands of Bach's students (notably Johann Tobias Krebs) bear so few fingerings that it would be imprudent to base any assumptions on them.

6. Statements by Bach's pupils and, to a lesser degree, "grandpupils" (i. e., pupils of pupils) concerning precepts of keyboard technique taught them by J. S. Bach. These are found in Volumes 2 and 3 of *Bach-Dokumente*[6] (hereinafter referred to as *Bach-Dokumente 2* or *3*), translated for the most part in the *Bach Reader*[7] (hereinafter referred to as *Bach Reader*; these translations are very accurate and reliable).

C. OTHER SECONDARY SOURCE MATERIAL

(Which has proved valuable in that it corroborates and amplifies the ideas presented in sources from within Bach's immediate circle):

1. Writings by J. S. Bach's immediate contemporaries (some of whom were acquainted with him) and men of the generation immediately following his. Into this category fall men such as Johann Mattheson, Johann Joachim Quantz, and Friedrich Wilhelm Marpurg.

2. Other treatises on aspects of music in general, and especially on keyboard technique, that were current during Bach's lifetime.

---

[5]Ed. Hans T. David and Arthur Mendel (New York: W. W. Norton, 1966), pp. 295—356. The English translation is that first published in England in 1820; it is remarkably precise, and it has been necessary to alter only an occasional word whose meaning has changed slightly in the course of time.

[6]Kassel: Bärenreiter, 1969, 1972.

[7]See note 5.

Position and Use of Fingers, Hands, and Body

A. A FLAWLESS TECHNIQUE

Das ist eben nichts bewundernswürdiges, man darf nur die rechten Tasten zu rechter Zeit treffen, so spielt das Instrument selbst.

There is nothing so remarkable about it; one need only hit the right keys at the right time, and the instrument plays itself.—J. S. Bach on his organ playing, quoted by J. F. Köhler after 1776 (*Bach-Dokumente 3*, p. 315; *Bach Reader*, p. 291).

Es kann seyn, dass mancher berühmter Mann in der Vollstimmigkeit auf diesen Instrumenten sehr viel geleistet hat: ist er deswegen eben so fertig, und zwar in Händen und Füssen zugleich, so fertig als Bach gewesen? Wer das Vergnügen gehabt hat, ihn und andere zu hören, und sonst nicht von Vorurtheilen eingenommen ist, wird diesen Zweifel nicht für ungegründet halten. Und wer Bachens Orgel und Clavierstücke, die er, wie überall bekannt ist, in der grösten Volkommenheit selbst ausführte, ansieht, wird ebenfalls nicht viel wider den obigen Satz einzuwenden haben.... Alle Finger waren bey ihm gleich geübt; Alle waren zu der feinsten Reinigkeit in der Ausführung gleich geschickt.

It may be that many a famous man has accomplished a great deal in polyphony upon these instruments [i. e., keyboard instruments]; did he therefore become equally as skillful in both hands and feet—as skillful as Bach was? Anyone who has had the pleasure of hearing both him and others, and has not been deceived by prejudice, will not consider this doubt ill-founded. Anyone who looks at Bach's organ and keyboard pieces, which, as is generally known, he himself performed with the greatest perfection, will likewise not find much to object to in the sentence above.... All his fingers were equally skillful; all were equally capable of the most perfect accuracy in performance.—From the "Nekrolog auf Johann Sebastian Bach," written in 1754 by C. P. E. Bach and Johann Friedrich Agricola (*Bach-Dokumente 3*, p. 88; *Bach Reader*, p. 223).

...entstand zuletzt ein so hoher Grad von Fertigkeit und (man könnte fast sagen) Allgewalt über das Instrument in allen Tonarten, dass es nun für Seb. Bach fast keine Schwierigkeiten mehr gab. So wohl bey seinen freyen Fantasien, als beym Vortrag seiner Compositionen, in welchen bekanntlich alle Finger beyder Hände ununterbrochen beschäftigt sind, und so fremdartige ungewöhnliche Bewegungen machen müssen, als die Melodien derselben selbst fremdartig und ungewöhnlich sind, soll er doch eine solche Sicherheit gehabt haben, dass er nie einen Ton verfehlte.

...Sebastian Bach at length acquired such a high degree of facility and, we may almost say, unlimited power over his instrument in all the keys that difficulties almost ceased to exist for him. As well in his unpremeditated fantasies as in executing his compositions (in which it is well known that all the fingers of both hands are constantly employed, and have to make motions which are as strange and uncommon as the melodies themselves), he is said to have possessed such certainty that he never missed a note.—Forkel, p. 16 (*Bach Reader*, p. 310).

Er ist ein ausserordentlicher Künstler auf dem Clavier und auf der Orgel.... Ich habe diesen grossen Mann unterschiedene mahl spielen hören. Man erstaunet bey seiner Fertigkeit, und man kan kaum begreifen, wie es möglich ist, dass er seine Finger und seine Füsse so sonderbahr und so behend in einander schrencken, ausdehnen, und damit die weitesten Sprünge machen kan, ohne einen einzigen falschen Thon einzumischen....

He is an extraordinary artist on the keyboard and on the organ.... I have heard this great man play on various occasions. One is amazed at his facility and one can hardly comprehend how it is possible for him to cross and extend over each other his fingers and his feet so peculiarly and nimbly, and thereby to execute the most extreme leaps without mixing in a single wrong tone....—From Johann Adolph Scheibe's deprecatory remarks on J. S. Bach's style of composition, published in the May 14, 1737, issue of Scheibe's *Critischer Musicus* (*Bach-Dokumente 2*, p. 286; *Bach Reader*, p. 238).

B. A QUIET TECHNIQUE

Bach, der grosse Joh. Seb. Bach, hat, wie alle, die ihn gehöret haben, einmüthiglich versichern, niemals die geringste Verdrehung des Körpers gemacht; man hat kaum seine Finger sich bewegen sehen....

Bach, the great Joh. Seb. Bach, as all who heard him unanimously affirm, never made the slightest contortion of his body; one could hardly see his fingers moving....—J. P. Kirnberger in Sulzer's *Allgemeine Theorie der Schönen Künste*, 1774 (*Bach-Dokumente 3*, p. 215).

...Versteht er die wahre Applicatur, so wird er, wenn er anders sich nicht unnöthige Gebehrden angewöhnt hat, die schweresten Sachen so spielen, dass man kaum die Bewegung der Hände siehet....

...If he [the performer] understands the correct principles of fingering and has not acquired the habit of making unnecessary gestures, he will then play the most difficult things in such a way that one hardly notices the motion of his hands....—C. P. E. Bach, *Versuch*, p. 18 (Mitchell, p. 43).

Auch soll Seb. Bach mit einer so leichten und kleinen Bewegung der Finger gespielt haben, dass man sie kaum bemerken konnte. Nur die vordern Gelenke der Finger waren in Bewegung, die Hand behielt auch bey den schwersten Stellen ihre gerundete Form, die Finger hoben sich nur wenig von den Tasten auf, fast nicht mehr als bey Trillerbewegungen, und wenn der eine zu thun hatte, blieb der andere in seiner ruhigen Lage. Noch weniger nahmen die übrigen Theile seines Körpers Antheil an seinem Spielen, wie es bey vielen geschieht, deren Hand nicht leicht genug gewöhnt ist.... Wenn er starke Affekten ausdrücken wollte, that er es nicht wie manche andere durch eine übertriebene Gewalt des Anschlags, sondern durch harmonische und melodische Figuren, das heisst: durch innere Kunstmittel.

Seb. Bach is said to have played with so easy and small a motion of the fingers that it was hardly perceptible. Only the first joints of the fingers were in motion; the hand retained even in the most difficult passages its rounded form; the fingers rose very little from the keys, hardly more than in a trill, and when one was employed, the other remained quietly in its position. Still less did the other parts of his body take any share in his play, as happens with many whose hand is not light enough.... When he wished to express strong emotions, he did not do it, as many do, by striking the keys with great force, but by melodical and harmonical figures, that is, by the internal resources of the art.—Forkel, pp. 13—14, 17—18 (*Bach Reader*, pp. 308, 312).

...Man kan kaum begreifen, wie es möglich ist, dass er seine Finger und seine Füsse...in einander schrencken [&] ausdehnen...kan...ohne...durch eine so heftige Bewegung den Körper zu verstellen.

...One can hardly comprehend how it is possible for him to cross and extend...his fingers and feet...without...displacing his body by any violent movement.—J. A. Scheibe, *Critischer Musicus*, 1737 (*Bach-Dokumente 2*, p. 286; *Bach Reader*, p. 238).

In addition to the obvious benefits to ease and facility in performance, a quiet technique keeps the body and head motionless and therefore allows the focus of the eyes upon the music to remain undisturbed. It also contributes to the maintenance of the performer's equilibrium and thus allows upcoming notes to be prepared by placing the requisite fingers over the keys in advance of the attack, as C. P. E. Bach seems to suggest:

Man gewöhne besonders die noch nicht ausgewachsenen Hände der Kinder, dass sie, anstatt des Hin- und Her-Springens mit der gantzen Hand, wobey wohl noch offt dazu die Finger auf einen Klumpen zusammen gezogen sind, die Hände im nöthigen Falle so viel möglich ausdehnen. Hierdurch werden sie die Tasten leichter und gewisser treffen lernen, und die Hände nicht leichte aus ihrer ordentlichen und über der Tastatur horizontal-schwebenden Lage bringen....Man muss bey dem Spielen beständig auf die Folge sehen, indem diese oft Ursache ist, dass wir andere als die gewöhnlichen Finger nehmen müssen.

One ought especially to train children's hands, not yet fully grown, to stretch as far as possible where necessary, rather than leap about with the entire hand, often drawing the fingers together into a clump. In this manner they will learn to strike the keys more easily and accurately, and not readily remove their hands from their proper position, hovering horizontally over the keyboard.... While playing one must constantly look ahead to approaching notes, since these often cause us to modify usual fingerings.—*Versuch*, pp.19—20 (Mitchell, pp. 43—44).

J. S. Bach's preference for the clavichord as an instrument for practice and for the formation of technique (as reported by Forkel, p. 17; *Bach Reader*, p. 311) is also indicative of a quiet technique; it is extremely difficult to control the tone of this instrument in any other way.[8] We know from the account of the distribution of Bach's estate (*Bach-Dokumente 2*, p. 504; *Bach Reader*, p. 197) that he possessed three "claviers" (probably clavichords—perhaps capable of being stacked one atop the other to create three manuals?) with a set of pedals.

C. POSITION OF HANDS AND FINGERS

Man spielt mit gebogenen Fingern und schlaffen Nerven; je mehr insgemein hierinnen gefehlt wird, desto nöthiger ist hierauf acht zu haben. Die Steiffe ist aller Bewegung hinderlich, besonders dem Vermögen, die Hände geschwind auszudehnen und zusammen zu ziehen, welches alle Augenblicke nöthig ist. Alle Spannungen, das Auslassen gewisser Finger, das Einsetzen zweyer Finger nach einander auf einen Ton, selbst das unentbehrliche Ueberschlagen und Untersetzen erfordert diese elastische Kraft. Wer mit ausgestreckten Fingern und steifen Nerven spielt, erfährt ausser der natürlich erfolgenden Ungeschicklichkeit, noch einen Haupt-Schaden, nehmlich er entfernt die übringen Finger wegen ihrer Länge zu weit von dem Daumen, welcher doch so nahe als möglich beständig bey der

Hand seyn muss....Es versteht sich von selbst, dass bey Sprüngen und weiten Spannungen diese Schlappigkeit der Nerven und das Gebogene der Finger nicht beybehalten werden kan; selbst das Schnellen erfordert bisweilen auf einen Augenblick eine Steiffe. Weil dieses aber die seltnesten Vorfälle sind, und welche die Natur von selbst lehret...

One should play with arched fingers and relaxed muscles. The less these two conditions are satisfied, the more attention must be given to them. Stiffness hampers all movement, above all the constantly required ability to extend and contract the hands rapidly. All stretches, the omission of certain fingers, the substitution of one finger for another on a note, even the indispensable crossing of the fingers and turning of the thumb demand this elastic ability. Those who play with flat, extended fingers and stiff muscles suffer from one principal disadvantage in addition to an inevitable awkwardness; the fingers, because of their length, are too far removed from the thumb, which must always remain as close as possible to the hand....It is evident that the muscles cannot remain relaxed nor the fingers arched in leaps or wide stretches; and even the *Schnellen* [an ornament] calls for a momentary tension. These are, however, the rarest cases and take care of themselves by their very nature....—*Versuch*, pp. 18 & 19 (Mitchell, pp. 42—43).

Nach der Seb. Bachischen Art, die Hand auf dem Clavier zu halten, werden die fünf Finger so gebogen, dass die Spitzen derselben in eine gerade Linie kommen, die sodann auf die in einer Fläche neben einander liegenden Tasten so passen, dass kein einziger Finger bey vorkommenden Fällen erst näher herbey gezogen muss, sondern dass jeder über dem Tasten, den er etwa nieder drücken soll, schon schwebt. Mit dieser Lage der Hand ist nun verbunden: 1) dass kein Finger auf seinen Tasten fallen, oder (wie es ebenfalls oft geschieht) geworfen, sondern nur mit einem gewissen Gefühl der innern Kraft und Herrschaft über die Bewegung getragen werden darf....

Die Vortheile einer solchen Haltung der Hand und eines solchen Anschlags sind sehr mannigfaltig, nicht bloss auf dem Clavichord, sondern auch auf dem Pianoforte und auf der Orgel.... 1) Die gebogene Haltung der Finger macht jede ihrer Bewegungen leicht. Das Hacken, Poltern und Stolpern kann also nicht entstehen, welches man so häufig bey Personen findet, die mit ausgestreckten oder nicht genug gebogenen Fingern spielen.

According to Sebastian Bach's manner of placing the hand on the keys, the five fingers are bent so that their tips come into a straight line,

---

[8]Jean-Claude Zehnder discusses the central role of the clavichord as a practice instrument in his article "Organ Articulation in the Seventeenth and Eighteenth Centuries," Part II, *The American Organist*, Vol. 17, No. 12 (December 1983), p. 43.

and so fit the keys, which lie in a plane surface under them, that no single finger has to be drawn nearer when it is wanted, but every one already hovers over the key which it may have to press down. What follows from this manner of holding the hand is: 1) that no finger must fall upon its key, or (as so often happens) be thrown on it, but only needs to be placed upon it with a certain consciousness of the internal power and command over the motion....

The advantages of such a position of the hand and such an attack are very various, not only on the clavichord, but also on the pianoforte and the organ.... 1) The holding of the fingers bent renders all their motions easy. There can therefore be none of the chopping, thumping, and stumbling which is so common in persons who play with their fingers stretched out, or not sufficiently bent.—Forkel, pp. 12—13 (*Bach Reader*, pp. 307— 08).

...Allerdings ist es gut, wenn die Claviere so kurz als möglich sind. Den wenn deren drey oder vier sind, so kann der Spielende, wenn die Claviere kurz sind, mit viel mehr Bequemlichkeit von einem auf dass andere kommen.... Wer einer richtigen Fingersetzung gewohnt ist, wird wissen, dass er keinen Finger in Spielen gerade ausstrecken muss. Wozu braucht er denn die so langen Claviere?...Die Semitone müssen überhaupt oben etwas schmäler als unten seyn. So verlangte sie der seel. Kapellm. Bach, welcher auch aus oben angeführten Ursachen, die kurzen Tasten auf Orgeln liebte.

...It is good to have the keyboards [i. e., the length of the key] as short as possible. For when there are three or four of them, the player can go from one to the other with much more ease if the manuals are short.... Anyone who is in the habit of placing his fingers properly will know that he need never stretch a finger out straight in playing. Why then does he need such long keys?...The semitones [accidentals] must generally be a little narrower at the top than at the bottom. That is how the late Kapellmeister Bach required them to be; he, for the above-mentioned reasons, also liked short keys on the organ.—Johann Friedrich Agricola (a student of Bach) in Adlung's *Musica Mechanica Organoedi*, 1768, pp. 23—24 (*Bach-Dokumente 3*, p. 193; *Bach Reader*, pp. 258—59).

Forkel's recommendation that all fingers should rest in a straight line and Agricola's advocacy of short-length keys are both related to the maintenance of a quiet technique, in which all fingers hover upon the keys at all times.

It is interesting to note in this connection the shape of Bach's hand and fingers. The two incontestably genuine portraits of Bach, painted by Elias Gottlieb Haussmann in 1746 and 1748, both portray Bach's right hand quite clearly.[9] The hand appears rather large and broad, and the fingers are quite fleshy and not particularly long. This visual record lends credence to the following statement (whose author's connection with the Bachs, however, is uncertain):

...Ich für mein Theil, ob mir gleich die Natur selbst lange Finger gegeben hat, halte die breitern Hände mit kürzern Fingern für vorzüglicher. Denn erstens ist es in den meisten Fällen gewiss, dass diese Hände am weitesten spannen. Erinnern Sie sich an das, was Sebastian und Emanuel Bach...mit solchen Händen geleistet haben.

...I for my part, although nature has given me long fingers, consider broader hands with shorter fingers to be superior. For in the first place it is certain that in most instances these hands have the widest span. Keep in mind that Sebastian and Emanuel Bach...had this sort of hands to work with.—L. A. L. Siebigk(e) (?), *Schlesische Provinzblätter*, 1800 (*Bach-Dokumente 3*, p. 565).

D. MOTION OF FINGERS

Man muss aber bey Ausführung der laufenden Noten, die Finger nicht so gleich wieder aufheben; sondern die Spitzen derselben vielmehr, auf dem vordersten Theil des Tasts hin, nach sich zurücke ziehen, bis sie vom Taste abgleiten. Auf diese Art werden die laufenden Passagien am deutlichsten herausgebracht. Ich berufe mich hierbey auf das Exempel eines der allergrössten Clavierspieler, der es so ausübte, und lehrete.

In the execution of running notes one must not lift the fingers immediately, but rather draw back the tips of them towards one over the most forward portion of the keys, until they glide off the key. In this way running passages may be brought out most clearly. In this connection I call attention to the example of one of the greatest of all keyboard players [here Quantz is referring to Bach, as his index shows], who followed this practice and taught it.—Johann Joachim Quantz, *Versuch einer Anweisung die Flöte traversiere zu spielen*, 1752 (*Bach-Dokumente 3*, p. 18; *Bach Reader*, p. 444).

[9]Reproduced in *Johann Sebastian Bach: Life/Times/Influence*, ed. Barbara Schwendowius and Wolfgang Dömling (Kassel: Barenreiter, 1977), pp. 6 & 61.

...Die...auf den Tasten getragene Kraft, oder das Maass des Drucks muss in gleicher Stärke unterhalten werden, und zwar so, dass der Finger nicht gerade aufwärts vom Tasten gehoben wird, sondern durch ein allmähliges Zurückziehen der Fingerspitzen nach der innern Fläche der Hand, auf dem vordern Theil des Tasten abgleitet.

...Beym Uebergange von einem Tasten zum andern wird durch dieses Abgleiten das Mass von Kraft oder Druck, womit der erste Ton unterhalten worden ist, in der grössten Geschwindigkeit auf den nächsten Finger geworfen, so dass nun die beyden Töne weder von einander gerissen werden, noch in einander klingen können.

...Das Einziehen der Fingerspitzen nach sich, und das dadurch bewirkte geschwinde Uebertragen der Kraft des einen Fingers auf den zunächst darauf folgenden, bringt den höchsten Grad von Deutlichkeit im Anschlage der einzelnen Töne hervor, so dass jede auf diese Art vorgetragene Passage glänzend, rollend und rund klingt, gleichsam als wenn jeder Ton eine Perle wäre....Durch das Gleiten der Fingerspitze auf dem Tasten in einerley Mass von Druck wird der Saite gehörige Zeit zum Vibriren gelassen; der Ton wird also dadurch nicht nur verschönert, sondern auch verlängert, und wir werden dadurch in den Stand gesetzt, selbst auf einem so Tonarmen Instrument, wie das Clavichord ist, sangbar und zusammenhängend spielen zu können.

...The impulse...given to the keys, or the quantity of pressure, must be maintained in equal strength, and that in such a manner that the finger not be raised perpendicularly from the key, but that it glide off the forepart of the key, by gradually drawing back the tip of the finger towards the palm of the hand.

...In the transition from one key to another, this gliding off causes the quantity of force or pressure with which the first tone has been kept up to be transferred with the greatest rapidity to the next finger, so that the two tones are neither disjoined from each other nor blended together.

...The drawing back of the tips of the fingers and the rapid communication, thereby effected, of the force of one finger to that following it produces the highest degree of clearness in the attack of the single tones, so that every passage performed in this manner sounds brilliant, rolling, and round, as if each tone were a pearl.

...By the gliding of the tip of the finger upon the key with an equable pressure, sufficient time is given to the string to vibrate; the tone, therefore, is not only improved, but also prolonged, and we are thus enabled to play in a singing style and with proper connection, even on an instrument so poor in tone as the clavichord is.—Forkel, pp. 12—13 (*Bach Reader*, pp. 307—08).

Forkel takes C. P. E. Bach to task for not describing in detail this aspect of his father's technique,[10] which Forkel nevertheless credits C. P. E. Bach with possessing. It is impossible to know the source of Forkel's very precise information on this gliding manner of release; surely it cannot be based entirely on Quantz's brief mention of it in 1752. It is possible that Forkel received it from C. P. E. Bach, perhaps even more likely from Wilhelm Friedemann Bach. At any rate, we are left with the puzzling fact that C. P. E. Bach does not mention it in the *Versuch*.

It is intriguing to speculate as to why the younger Bach did not transmit his father's instruction on this matter. It can hardly have been because he had forgotten it, especially considering that Forkel expressly states that Emanuel Bach practiced it. The only other possible conclusion is that C. P. E. Bach did not consider it of sufficient import or relevance to include in the *Versuch*. It is within the realm of credibility to conjecture that C. P. E. Bach's disregard of this principle arose from his almost exclusive cultivation of the clavichord and his neglect of the organ.[11] This type of finger motion finds its greatest value in the control of the release of each note. And, Forkel's comments notwithstanding, the precise control of the release of a tone is far more crucial to organ technique than to that of keyboard string instruments. Indeed, a thorough command of the release of tones is above all important in the performance of densely contrapuntal works, in which each line must be executed independently of the others and with the greatest clarity. It is also possible, of course, that Emanuel Bach, recognizing the considerable effort necessary to master this technique, simply decided to omit mention of it for purely practical reasons. Perhaps he considered it so advanced a practice that only a few highly skilled players could ever benefit from incorporating it into their technique, or perhaps even a sort of "trade secret"

---

[10]P. 12 (*Bach Reader*, p. 307).

[11]He told Charles Burney that he had neglected the organ so long that he had lost his skill on the pedals. See Charles Burney, *The Present State of Music in Germany, the Netherlands, and United Provinces*, Vol. II (London: Backet, 1773), p. 274.

to be passed on to the initiated only by word of mouth. At any rate, his silence on the matter is a startling gap in an otherwise thoroughly systematic record.

E. EQUAL SKILLFULNESS OF FINGERS

Alle Finger waren bey ihm gleich geübt....
All his fingers were equally skillful....—"Nekrolog," 1754 (*Bach-Dokumente 3*, p. 88; *Bach Reader*, p. 309).

Der natürliche Unterschied der Finger an Grösse, so wie an Stärke, verleitet sehr häufig die Clavierspieler, sich da, wo es nur irgend möglich ist, bloss der stärkern zu bedienen, und die schwächern zu vernachlässigen. Dadurch entsteht nicht nur eine Ungleichheit im Anschlage mehrerer auf einander folgender Töne, sondern sogar eine Unmöglichkeit, gewisse Sätze, wobey keine Auswahl der Finger Statt findet, heraus zu bringen. Joh. Seb. fühlte diess bald, und um einer so fehlerhaften Bildung abzuhelfen, schrieb er sich besondere Stücke, wobey die Finger beyder Hände in den mannigfaltigsten Lagen nothwendig alle gebraucht werden mussten, wenn sie rein heraus gebracht werden sollten. Durch solche Uebungen bekamen alle seine Finger beyder Hände gleiche Stärke und Brauchbarkeit, so dass er nicht nur Doppelgriffe und alles Laufwerk mit beyden Händen, sondern auch einfache und Doppeltriller mit gleicher Leichtigkeit und Feinheit auszuführen vermochte. Sogar solche Sätze hatte er in seiner Gewalt, worin, während einige Finger trillern, die übrigen derselben Hand eine Melodie fortzuführen haben.

The natural difference between the fingers in size as well as strength frequently seduces performers, wherever it can be done, to use only the stronger fingers and neglect the weaker ones. Hence arises not only an inequality in the attack of several successive tones, but even the impossibility of executing certain passages where no choice of fingers can be made. Joh. Seb. was soon sensible of this; and, to obviate so great a defect in technique, wrote for himself particular pieces, in which all the fingers of both hands must necessarily be employed in the most various positions in order to perform them properly and distinctly. By these exercises he rendered all his fingers, of both hands, equally strong and serviceable, so that he was able to execute not only chords and all running passages, but also single and double trills with equal ease and delicacy. He was perfectly master even of those passages in which, while some fingers perform a trill, the others, on the same hand, have to continue the melody.—Forkel, p. 14 (*Bach Reader*, p. 309).

Das erste, was er hierbey that, war, seine Schüler die ihm eigene Art des Anschlags, von welcher schon geredet worden ist, zu lehren. Zu diesem Behuf mussten sie mehrere Monathe hindurch nichts als einzelne Sätze für alle Finger beyder Hände, mit steter Rücksicht auf diesen deutlichen und saubern Anschlag, üben. Unter einigen Monathen konnte keiner von diesen Uebungen loskommen, und seiner Ueberzeugung nach hätten sie wenigstens 6 bis 12 Monathe lang fortgesetzt werden müssen. Fand sich aber, dass irgend einem derselben nach einigen Monathen die Geduld ausgehen wollte, so war er so gefällig, kleine zusammenhängende Stücke vorzuschreiben, worin jene Uebungssätze in Verbindung gebracht waren. Von dieser Art sind die 6 kleinen Präludien für Anfänger, und noch mehr die 15 zweystimmigen Inventionen.

The first thing he did was to teach his students his peculiar mode of touching the instrument, of which we have spoken before [see p. 18—19 above]. For this purpose, he made them practice, for months together, nothing but isolated exercises for all the fingers of both hands, with constant regard to this clear and clean touch. For a number of months, none could get excused from these exercises; and, according to his firm opinion, they ought to be continued, at least, for from 6 to 12 months. But if he found that anyone, after some months of practice, began to lose patience, he was so obliging as to write little connected pieces, in which those exercises were combined together. Of this kind are the 6 little Preludes for Beginners, and still more the 15 two-part Inventions.—Forkel, p. 38 (*Bach Reader*, p. 328).

The "isolated exercises for all the fingers of both hands" have unfortunately not been preserved. They may indeed never have been written down, being communicated solely by oral instruction from teacher to pupil.

Fingering

Concerning J.S. Bach's early keyboard training we know very little:

Johann Sebastian war noch nicht zehen Jahr alt, als er sich, seiner Eltern durch den Tod beraubet sahe. Er begab sich nach Ohrdruff zu seinem ältesten Bruder Johann Christoph, Organisten daselbst, und legte unter desselben Anführung den Grund zum Clavierspielen.

Johann Sebastian was not yet ten years old when he found himself bereft of his parents by death. He betook himself to Ohrdruff, where his eldest brother Johann Christoph was organist, and under this brother's guidance he laid the foundation for his keyboard playing.—"Nekrolog," 1754 (*Bach-Dokumente 3*, p. 81; *Bach Reader*, p. 216).

...Ausser Frobergern, Kerl u. Pachhelbel hat er die Wercke von Frescobaldi, dem Badenschen Capellmeister Fischer, Strunck, einigen alten guten französischen, Buxdehude, Reincken, Bruhnsen u. dem Lüneburgischen Organisten Böhmen geliebt u. studiert.

...Besides Froberger, Kerl and Pachhelbel, he loved and studied the works of Frescobaldi, the Baden Capellmeister Fischer, Strunck, some old and good Frenchmen, Buxdehude, Reincken, Bruhns and [crossed out: his teacher Böhm] the Lüneburg organist Böhm.—From a letter of C. P. E. Bach to J. N. Forkel, Jan. 13, 1775 (*Bach-Dokumente 3*, p. 288; *Bach Reader*, p. 278).

Thus in keyboard performance (as in composition) J. S. Bach was apparently largely self-taught. At any rate, discounting whatever study he may have had with Georg Böhm (which cannot have been extensive), he seems never to have studied with a well-known keyboard performer. His mind was, however, remarkably open to all the musical activity surrounding him, and the fingering practices he learned during his formative years were unquestionably related to the early keyboard fingering methods prevalent in Germany during his childhood and youth (BWV 994 stands as witness to this).

A. THE PRIMARY SOURCES

The *Applicatio*

The beginning of any investigation of Bach's fingering practices must entail an examination of the two autograph pieces in the *Clavier-büchlein vor Wilhelm Friedemann Bach*. Since these pieces are rather different in texture, it is not surprising that they exhibit different facets of Bach's fingering practice. The *Applicatio* (BWV 994; see facsimile, p. 25 below) is an exercise piece, written basically to show the usual method of performing scale passages. It is not musically complex, nor is it technically difficult (except for the ornaments employing the fourth and fifth fingers of the right hand; see in this regard the quotations on the previous page, concerning the equal skillfulness of Bach's fingers). The scale pat-

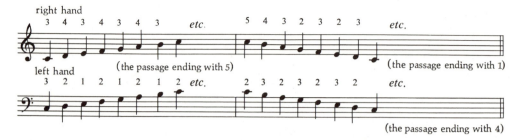

right hand
3 4 3 4 3 4 3 *etc.* (the passage ending with 5) 5 4 3 2 3 2 3 *etc.* (the passage ending with 1)

left hand
3 2 1 2 1 2 1 2 *etc.* 2 3 2 3 2 3 2 *etc.* (the passage ending with 4)

terns employed in this piece are those common in Germany throughout the 17th and early 18th centuries, in which a longer finger must alternate with a shorter one by vaulting it: right hand 343434 ascending and 323232 descending; left hand 121212 ascending.[12]

Fingering patterns similar to these are prescribed in Johann Mattheson's *Kleine general-bass-schule* (Hamburg, 1735). On page 72 of this publication Mattheson describes in writing the proper fingering for scales, which is notated above:

This source agrees with the *Applicatio* as to the correct fingering for three scales (right hand ascending and descending; left hand ascending), and it also provides a fingering for the left-hand descending scale. Bach may have omitted an example of this scale fingering because of the variety of fingerings apparently allowed for it: e. g., BB Mus. Ms. P801, p. 171 (in the hand of J. G. Walther), *Fugue in B minor* on a theme of Albinoni, BWV 951, employs the thumb and index finger in alterna-

3 4 5

2 1 2 1 2 1 2 1   2 1   2 3

tion, while the *Fugetta*, BWV 870a (m. 31, bass, beat 4), hints at the possibility of alternation between the third and fourth fingers.[13]

The *Applicatio* makes it clear that Bach was grounded in the earlier fingering practices and that he still considered them valid and

useful. It is unlikely that the fingerings it proposes represent an early stage of development for J. S. Bach (one that he later abandoned), since the *Clavier-büchlein vor Wilhelm Friedemann Bach* postdates most of Bach's mature keyboard works (including, for example, all of the great Weimar organ works). Furthermore, Friedemann Bach did not forget or reject this fingering method; Daniel Gottlob Türk writes:

Der verstorbene Friedemann Bach (ehedem in Halle), unstreitig einer der grössten und gründlichsten Orgelspieler, die damals in Deutschland lebten, soll mit diesen beyden Fingern, wie man hier allgemein behauptet, gewisse Läufer rund und mit einer erstaunenswürdigen Geschwindigkeit heraus gebracht haben.

The deceased Friedemann Bach (formerly in Halle [Türk's home]), indisputably one of the greatest and most able organists who formerly lived in Germany, is reported to have performed certain passages roundly and with amazing speed with these two fingers [3 & 4], as is generally attested here [in Halle].— Daniel Gottlob Türk, *Klavierschule* (Leipzig und Halle: Schwickert, 1789), p. 148.

The *Praeambulum*

This piece (BWV 930; see facsimile, p. 26 below) is the least helpful in determining Bach's fingering practice. It is more contrapuntal in texture than the *Applicatio*, but the counterpoint, except for the closing measures of each of the two sections, is in only two voices. Furthermore, the entire piece consists of arpeggiated chords, whose fingering is basically that still employed by keyboard performers today. The *Praeambulum* exhibits in several instances a few of Bach's practices that differ from modern ones (e.g., mm. 22—23, soprano; mm. 34—35, bass), but on the whole neither this work nor the *Applicatio* offers substantial aid in determining the fingering Bach used for four-voice counterpoint.

---

[12]The left-hand pattern is the reverse of that found in some other examples of early fingering practice, in which the second finger is placed on the strong beat. No great significance should be attached to this variation. The pattern is one that approaches the modern thumb-under fingering method; it need not have any effect on articulation, as do most earlier fingering patterns. In this particular instance it should be viewed as a practical solution to the problem at hand; it allows the thumb to arrive, as needed, on the highest note of the scale, preparatory to the ensuing downward leap of an octave. In the *Prelude*, BWV 870a, the thumb is also used in this way, yet it appears on off-beats as well (BWV 870a, *Fugetta*, bass, mm. 28—29).

[13]The *Wegweiser*—by Johann Speth (?); Augsburg, 1689, Part I—also prefers this latter fingering for the left-hand descending scale: 343434.

B. DECISIVE SECONDARY SOURCES

The *Prelude & Fugetta in C Major*

The fingering indications found in this work (BWV 870a; see score, pp. 27—29 below) probably transmit Bach's intentions, even though the manuscript is not in his own hand.[14] These pieces are thoroughly contrapuntal, the *Prelude* having four voices, the *Fugetta* having three. This source, then, imparts a more complete picture of how Bach's students may have been taught to finger his greatest works, e. g., the preludes and fugues of *Das wohltemperierte Clavier*, the keyboard suites, and the preludes, fugues, and chorale settings for organ. A thorough examination of this source reveals the following principles of fingering:

1. The equal use of all fingers. This is only to be expected in light of Bach's reported insistence on the equal skillfulness of all the fingers. In particular, there is a consistent use of the thumb of both hands, clearly differentiating Bach's practice from those earlier practices that avoided the thumb when possible.

2. The remarkably frequent use of the same finger on two notes in succession. A finger that is depressing one key is released, and by means of a tiny hop is transferred to another note which it immediately depresses. The outer fingers of each hand—the thumb and fifth finger—undertake this action far more frequently than the other fingers (e. g., *Prelude*, m. 14, soprano; m. 4, tenor), although all the fingers of both hands engage in it at one point or another. Normally this action occurs from note to adjacent note, but there are a number of instances in which it spans a leap of a third, a fourth, or even a fifth (e. g., *Fugetta*, mm. 8—9, alto).[15]

This action is actually a species of early fingering; examples of it can be found throughout the early literature that contains fingering. If this source uses it rather more frequently, it is due to the greater technical demands of the music. The action is best accomplished by a motion of the hand that is peculiar to early modes of fingering. In order to follow the finger in its course, the hand must execute sporadic, minute, and rapid lateral shifts. These shifts are accomplished with all fingers of the hand still basically in contact with the keys, and often allow the hand to retain the most natural position possible. This shift is not described in any of the sources from Bach's circle—it arises naturally as the most efficient way to accomplish any of the earlier fingering patterns (including scales) in which one finger vaults another.

3. The use of the thumb and fifth finger on an accidental is avoided whenever possible, although it does occur whenever it is the most convenient solution to the problem at hand. This limitation is in accord with C. P. E. Bach's instruction:

...der kleine Finger selten und die Daumen anders nicht als im Nothfalle solche [d. h., die halben Töne] berühren.
...Der Daumen bleibt von den halben Tönen weg, desgleichen der kleine Finger; ...wenn ein vorhergegangener oder nachfolgender Sprung dieses nothwendig macht.

...[Accidentals] are seldom taken by the little finger and only out of necessity by the thumb.
...The thumb avoids accidentals, as does the little finger...[except] when a contextual leap makes it necessary.—*Versuch*, pp. 22 & 37 (Mitchell, pp. 45 & 60).

4. Substitution of one finger for another on the same key is generally avoided. The only instance of substitution occurs in measure 25 of the *Fugetta*, on a pedal tone (this use of substitution is customarily allowed in early fingering practice[16]). This principle C. P. E. Bach also records:

Da dieses Hülffs-Mittel so gar leicht nicht ist, geschickt zu gebrauchen, so hat es von Rechts wegen nur bey einer wenigstens etwas langen Note und im Falle der Noth statt.

Because it is not easy to employ this device skillfully it is correctly restricted to relatively long notes and in cases of necessity.—*Versuch*, p. 45 (Mitchell, p. 72).

---

[14]The reliability of this source is supported by its similarity to the fingering in the Kirnberger source, discussed on the next two pages.

[15]It is instructive to note that these larger leaps invariably occur before beats one and three, i. e., the strong beats.

---

[16]Finger substitution on a note of longer duration is explicitly described by Gottlieb Muffat in the foreword to his *Componimenti Musicali* (ca. 1739).

He indeed criticizes Francois Couperin (*L'Art de toucher le clavecin*) for suggesting the use of substitution too frequently.[17] The use of substitution in the 19th and 20th centuries has never been as common among pianists as among organists (due in part to the legato effect that can be obtained through the use of the piano's damper pedal, and in part to the piano's relative freedom from an abrupt instant of release for each tone); there are in fact numerous instances of fingering in piano editions that call for the use of the same finger on two notes in succession, rather than substitution.[18]

5. The passing of the fingers over the thumb (i.e., the thumb's use as a pivot—the cardinal principle of modern fingering) is also found, though with no great frequency (e. g., *Fugetta*, mm. 28—33, bass); this alternation of thumb and index finger is also evident in the *Applicatio*.

6. When circumstances warrant, there appear some strikingly unusual fingerings which, when examined and tried, prove to be eminently sensible solutions to otherwise thorny problems. Such unusual fingerings are found both in the *Prelude* (m. 8, tenor, beat 2; m. 10, bass, beats 1 & 2) and in the *Fugetta* (mm. 27—28, bass). These solutions are best executed by shifting the hand in a rapid lateral motion as described above, on the previous page.

7. The early fingering practice of one finger vaulting another (analogous to that in the *Applicatio*) is also found, though it is not as conspicuous as the use of the same finger on two notes in succession. The most frequent early fingering pattern in the left hand is 1212 (*Prelude*, m. 5, bass), although other patterns are also found:

4 over 5: *Prelude*, m. 7, bass, beats 1—2;
5 under 4: *Prelude*, m. 9, bass, beats 2—3.

The patterns in the right hand that are derived from early fingering practices are both more diverse and more frequent:

2 over 3: *Prelude*, m. 15, soprano, beats 3—4;
2 over 5: *Prelude*, m. 7, soprano, beat 2;
3 over 4: *Prelude*, m. 11, soprano, beats 1—2;
3 over 5: *Fugetta*, m. 6, soprano, beats 1—2;
5 under 3: *Fugetta*, m. 10, soprano, beats 2—3,
      Prelude, mm. 6—7, soprano;
5 under 4: *Fugetta*, m. 20 , soprano, beats 2—3.

In each case, of course, it is the longer finger that crosses over or the shorter that crosses under. Note that these crossings occur in leaps as well as in stepwise motion. It would be impossible to systematize their use, since in each case they arise in response to the needs of the moment.

8. The *Fugetta* shows at three points (mm. 11—12, 13—19, and 26—27) the exchange of the middle voice from one hand to the other. The points of exchange are marked in the manuscript (see pp. 28—29 below) by a division line running through the treble staff. This division of labor between hands allows the smoothest performance of the voices.

Kirnberger's Fingering for the "Allabreve"

Kirnberger published his *Clavierübungen mit der Bachischen Applicatur* (Keyboard Studies with the Bach Fingering Method) as a companion to C. P. E. Bach's *Versuch*. The four collections under this title consist of pieces of progressive difficulty, almost all of which bear fingerings provided by Kirnberger. In his foreword the author recommends the use of the *Versuch* and states that the fingerings he has provided are based upon it. The pieces in the four collections are almost entirely short dances and other lighter pieces in the *galant* style then in fashion. These pieces are homophonically conceived, with sparse textures (either two or three voices), frequent rests, many arpeggiated figures, and rapid scales.

In sharp contrast to the *galant* pieces is the "Allabreve" found on pp. 14—15 of the third collection (see facsimile, p. 30). It is a fugue in the strict contrapuntal style of the late baroque era, varying in texture from two to four voices. Although Kirnberger denotes the composer as a "Mr. Holland," the work is in fact one of the Magnificat fugues by the composer Johann

[17] *Versuch*, p. 45 (Mitchell, p. 72).

[18] E. g., J. N. Hummel's fingering of the Fugue in C-sharp minor from *Das wohltemperierte Clavier* (BWV 849), in his *Anweisung zum Piano-Forte-Spiel* (Vienna: Tobias Haslinger [preface 1827]), pp. 379—81.

Pachelbel.[19] Unlike the other pieces in the collection, the indications "Man." and "Ped." under the lowest staff mark this one as intended for performance on the organ. The fingerings Kirnberger gives, however, make it possible to perform the work entirely on the manuals. Careful scrutiny is necessary to determine which notes are to be taken by which hand; once this has been accomplished, the fingerings are quite convenient and comfortable.

The conclusion that emerges from a careful analysis of this piece's fingering is that the principles which underlie it correspond with those behind the *Prelude & Fugetta* (BWV 870a). The frequent use of the same finger on two notes in succession (especially the outer fingers), the avoidance of substitution (only two instances, mm. 23 & 71, both on long note values), the occasional unusual fingerings (e. g., m. 30, soprano and alto)— all follow the same practices evident in BWV 870a. There is, to be sure, less evidence of the earlier practice of one finger vaulting another (though the alternation of thumb and index finger may be found, e. g., mm. 21—22, tenor); this is hardly surprising, however, in light of the publication's late date (1763, 13 years after Bach's death) and the piece's lesser technical difficulty. The correspondence of these two sources, written more than 30 years apart, renders them both all the more credible as authentic reflections of J. S. Bach's fingering practices.

---

[19]Magnificat primi toni I,No.15. Modern edition found in: *Denkmäler der Tonkunst in Oesterreich*, Vol. 17, p. 16.

Facsimiles of "Applicatio" and "Praeambulum" courtesy of Yale University, Music Library.

Prelude composeè par J.S. Bach
[BWV 870a]

*sic

[sic]

*sic

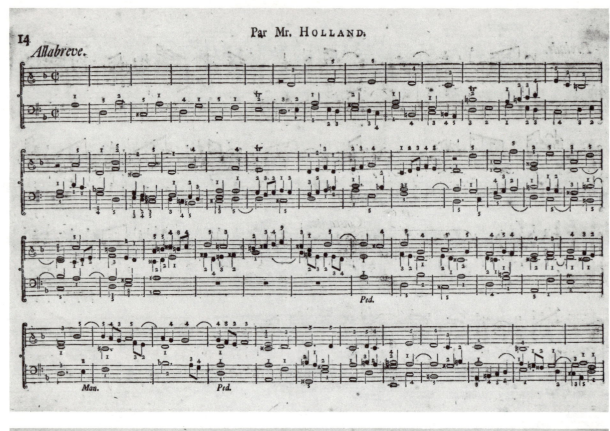

Facsimiles of the "Allabreve" courtesy of the Music Division, Library of Congress.

Fingering Information in C. P. E. Bach's *Versuch*

While his statements on performance practice may reflect ideas of a later age, in matters of fingering as well as of general keyboard technique the information C. P. E. Bach gives in his *Versuch* records essentially the practice he learned from his father. He states in his autobiography: "In composition and in keyboard performance I have never had another teacher than my father,"[20] and he also declares that the principles of fingering he expounds in the *Versuch* are those of his father.[21] Futhermore, his role as interpreter of his father's practices was never questioned by any of J. S. Bach's other sons or pupils; in fact, Forkel (who surely would have learned from W. F. Bach of any discrepancies between the teaching of Emanuel and his father) states that it is Emanuel who has explained his father's teachings on fingering.[22] In his foreword to the *Clavierübungen mit der Bachischen Applicatur*, J. P. Kirnberger, an ardent connoisseur as well as a student of J. S. Bach, supports Emanuel Bach's fingering method as the "easiest, most comfortable and most complete (see p. 10 above) and recommends that teachers and students become acquainted with the rules set forth in the *Versuch*. Daniel Gottlob Türk (a Bach grandpupil through G.A. Homilius) in his *Klavierschule* (p. 130) likewise recognizes Emanuel Bach as the transmitter and interpreter of his father's teachings on fingering. Finally, E. L. Gerber, whose father and teacher H. N. Gerber was a Bach pupil, affirms in his *Tonkünstler-Lexicon* that one may learn J. S. Bach's finger technique from the *Versuch*.[23] All the evidence, then, supports the claim that Emanuel Bach's statements on fingering are in essence those of his father. The *Versuch* is of decisive significance in arriving at a comprehensive conception of J. S. Bach's fingering practice.

Even cursory examination of the principles set forth in the *Versuch*, however, reveals that C. P. E. Bach's fingering concepts do not reflect the same emphases as those characteristic of the primary sources (nor, for that matter, of the secondary sources already discussed). This difference does not amount to an actual contradiction; rather, Emanuel offers his readers a somewhat different view of the matter. If this view differs from the one gleaned from the primary sources, then it is because Emanuel's statements on fingering had to be applied to works that were fundamentally different in texture and style from those of his father. In trying to understand Emanuel's fingering concepts as they relate to his father's, it is essential to remember that he was dealing with an older technique that now had to be put to the purposes of a new style. It then follows that certain aspects of the technique needed to be emphasized at the expense of others.

New Use of the Thumb

Emanuel Bach states the primary thrust of his report on his father's practice at the beginning of his chapter on fingering:

> Mein seeliger Vater hat mir erzählt, in seiner Jugend grosse Männer gehört zu haben, welche den Daumen nicht eher gebraucht, als wenn es bey grossen Spannungen nöthig war. Da er nun einen Zeitpunckt erlebt hatte, in welchem nach und nach eine gantz besondere Veränderung mit dem musicalischen Geschmack vorging: so wurde er dadurch genöthiget, einen weit vollkommnern Gebrauch der Finger sich auszudencken, besonders den Daumen....Da diese neue Finger-Setzung so beschaffen ist, das man damit alles mögliche zur bestimmten Zeit leicht herausbringen kan; so lege ich solche hier zum Grunde.

> My deceased father told me that in his youth he used to hear great men who employed their thumbs only when necessary in large stretches. Because he lived at a time when a gradual striking change in musical taste was taking place, he was obliged to devise a far more complete use of the fingers, especially the thumb....

> Because this new fingering is such that everything can be played easily with it at the proper time, I shall expound it here.—*Versuch*, p. 17 (Mitchell, p. 42).

This new use of the thumb Emanuel explains in precise detail later in the chapter. It consists principally in the ability of the thumb

[20] From *Carl Burney's...Tagebuch seiner Musikalischen Reisen...aus dem Englischen ubersetzt...*(by Johann Joachim Christoph Bode, who obtained from Emanuel an autobiography that he substituted for Burney's remarks on his life). Dritter Band (Hamburg: Bode, 1773), p. 199.

[21] *Versuch*, p. 17 (Mitchell, p. 42).

[22] P. 15 (*Bach Reader*, p. 310).

[23] E. L. Gerber, *Historisch-Biographisches Lexicon der Tonkünstler* (Leipzig: Breitkopf, 1790); *Bach-Dokumente 3*, p. 468.

to pass under the other fingers and thus to facilitate the performance of scales that extend beyond a five-note compass.[24] He gives a fundamental rule that should be observed in using the thumb:

> ...der Daumen der rechten Hand im Aufsteigen nach einem oder mehrern halben Tönen, im Absteigen aber vor einem oder mehrern halben Tönen, und der lincke Daumen im Absteigen nach, und im Aufsteigen vor den halben Tönen, eingesetzt wird.
>
> ...The thumb of the right hand is brought in after one or more accidentals in ascending, before one or more accidentals in descending, and the left thumb after accidentals in descending, and before them in ascending.—*Versuch*, p. 25 (Mitchell, p. 48).

a rule that was later amplified by J. P. Kirnberger:

> Mache man ihnen die von Joh. Seb. Bach erfundene Regel bekannt: dass in den meisten Fällen vor und nach dem Leitton (Semitonio modi), es falle solcher auf einen halben oder ganzen Ton, der Daum eingesetzet werde.
>
> One should make known to them [i.e., to children] the rule discovered by Joh. Seb. Bach: that in most cases the thumb should be inserted before and after the leading tone (semitonium modi), whether it falls on a half or a whole tone [i.e., on an accidental or a natural].—J. P. Kirnberger, *Grundsätze des General-Basses* (Berlin, 1781); *Bach-Dokumente 3*, p. 345 (*Bach Reader*, p. 450).

Emanuel Bach considers the mastery of this technique a hallmark of an accomplished performer:

> ...heisst dieses untersetzen. Uebt man sich so lange, biss der Daumen auf eine mechanische Art sich von selbst auf diese Weise am gehörigen Ort ein- und untersetzt; so hat man das meiste in der Finger-Setzung gewonnen.
>
> ...This [action of the thumb] is called passing under. One must practice until the thumb automatically passes under in this way at the proper place; thus does one gain the summit of fingering.—*Versuch*, p. 33 (Mitchell, p. 57).

Emanuel Bach does not claim that his father was the sole inventor of this new use of the thumb. Other keyboard players were during this same period experimenting with a similar use of the thumb as a pivot finger.[25] Indeed, the type of fingering specified for the left hand in earlier fingering systems (seen, e. g., in the *Applicatio*) is a species of incipient thumb-under fingering. It seems probable, however, that J. S. Bach was one of the first, if not *the* first, to use this technique extensively and to begin to consider how it could be applied systematically. Johann Tobias Krebs, one of J. S. Bach's earliest pupils (Weimar, before 1717), already knew and used this technique, as is evidenced by fingerings for the following right-hand scale passage. In BB Mus. Ms. P801, p. 125, these appear in Krebs' handwriting, probably written while Bach was still working in Weimar:

Increased Use of Accidentals

Emanuel Bach also gives the reason behind his father's effort in developing this new technique:

> ...So wurde er dadurch genöthiget, einen weit vollkommnern Gebrauch der Finger sich auszudencken, besonders den Daumen, welcher ausser andern guten Diensten hauptsächlich in den schweren Ton-Arten gantz unentbehrlich ist, so zu gebrauchen, wie ihn die Natur gleichsam gebrauchet wissen will....
>
> ...sie nur eine Art von Finger-Setzung haben, allwo der Daumen durch die Uebung in seinen ordentlichen Platz sich von selbst eindringen lernt. Diese letztern behalten den Nahmen der schweren nur aus der Ursache bey, weil entweder gar nicht, oder selten aus selbigen gespielt und gesetzt wird. Hierdurch bleibt ihre Schreib-Art so wohl als die Lage ihrer Tasten allezeit fremde. Durch die wahre Lehre und Anwendung der Finger-Ordnung werden uns also diese schwere Ton-Arten eben so leichte, als gross die Schwierigkeit war, auf eine falsche Art, besonders ohne Daumen oder den rechten Gebrauch desselben in solchen fort zu kommen. Einer der grösten Vorzüge des Claviers, vermöge dessen man mit besonderer Leichtigkeit aus allen vier-und-zwantzig

---

[24]P. 24 (Mitchell, pp. 45—46).

[25]E. g., Jean-Philippe Rameau, "De la Mechanique des Doigts sur le Clavessin" (in his *Pieces de Clavessin*, Paris, 1724), p. 5; also P. C. Humanus in his *Dess Musici Theoretico-Practici* (1749); see also Philipp Spitta, *Johann Sebastian Bach* (London: Novello, 1883—85), Vol. II, pp. 37—38; see also Jean-Claude Zehnder, "Organ Articulation in the Seventeenth and Eighteenth Centuries," p. 27 (re Prelleur and "the Italian manner of fingering").

Ton-Arten spielen kan, ist also durch die Unwissenheit der rechten Applicatur verborgen geblieben.

...He [J. S. Bach] was obliged to devise a far more complete use of the fingers and especially to enlarge the role of the thumb, which, aside from its other good services, is by nature absolutely indispensable in the difficult keys [i.e., keys with many accidentals]....

...These [i.e., keys with many accidentals] have only one method of fingering, in which the thumb through practice learns to find its proper place effortlessly. These keys are called difficult only because they are either never or rarely ever played or employed in their own right. As a result, their notation as well as the location of their keys remains always unfamiliar. Once forbidding, when they were incorrectly played without the thumb or the correct use of it, these difficult keys have become inviting, thanks to the true study and employment of the fingers. [In earlier times] one of the great advantages of the keyboard, the facility in which one can play in all twenty-four keys, lay hidden behind ignorance of proper fingering.—*Versuch*, pp. 17 & 34 (Mitchell, pp. 42 & 58).

Forkel echoes and amplifies Emanuel Bach's assertions:

Vor ihm und noch in seinen Jugendjahren, wurde mehr harmonisch als melodisch, auch noch nicht in allen 24 Tonarten gespielt. Weil das Clavier noch gebunden war, so dass mehrere Tasten unter eine einzige Saite schlugen, so konnte es noch nicht rein temperirt werden; man spielte also nur aus solchen Tonarten, die sich am reinsten stimmen liessen. Von diesen Umständen kam es, dass selbst die damahligen grössten Spieler den Daumen nicht eher gebrauchten, als bis er bey Spannungen durchaus unentbehrlich wurde. Da Bach nun anfing, Melodie und Harmonie so zu vereinigen, dass selbst seine Mittel-Stimmen nicht bloss begleiten, sondern ebenfalls singen mussten, da er den Gebrauch der Tonarten theils durch Abweichung von den damahls auch in der weltlichen Musik noch sehr üblichen Kirchentönen, theils durch Vermischung des diatonischen und chromatischen Klanggeschlechts erweiterte, und nun sein Instrument so temperiren lernte, dass es in allen 24 Tonarten rein gespielt werden konnte; so musste er sich auch eine andere, seinen neuen Einrichtungen angemessenere Fingersetzung ausdenken, und besonders den Daumen anders gebrauchen, als er bisher gebraucht worden war.

Before his [i. e., J. S. Bach's] time and in his younger years, it was usual to play rather harmony [i. e., counterpoint] than melody [i. e., homophony], and not in all the 24 major and minor keys. As the clavichord was still fretted, so that several keys struck a single string, it could not be perfectly tempered; people played therefore only in those keys which could be tuned with the most purity. Through these circumstances it happened that even the greatest performers of that time did not use the thumb till it was absolutely necessary in stretches. Now when Bach began to unite melody and harmony so that even his middle parts did not merely accompany, but had a melody of their own, when he extended the use of the keys, partly by deviating from the ancient modes of church music, partly by mixing the diatonic and chromatic scales, and learned to temper his instrument so that it could be played upon in all the 24 keys, he was at the same time obliged to contrive another mode of fingering, better adapted to his new methods, and particularly to use the thumb in a manner different from that hitherto employed.—Forkel, pp. 14— 15 (*Bach Reader*, p. 309).

In examining all of the above statements concerning the use of the thumb, two fundamental principles emerge. First, J. S. Bach taught that the thumb is employed to advantage especially in those situations where the presence of numerous accidentals renders the exclusive use of the other four fingers inadequate. Second, the use of the thumb as a pivot finger is particularly suited to the smooth execution of scale passages that extend beyond a five-note compass; more particularly, it facilitates performance of scales with many accidentals.

The use of the thumb as a pivot finger is found occasionally in the sources analyzed above (pp. 23—25), but it does not form a conspicuous feature of their fingering. We can now understand why this is so. These pieces are not in "difficult" keys; they employ only a limited number of accidentals. They seldom employ scale passages that move beyond a five-note compass, and none of the scales in them uses any more than an occasional accidental. Indeed, BWV 870a is a prime example of the late baroque compositional process so characteristic of J. S. Bach: It is made up of short motives or melodic cells, and does not depend on scale passages, which play so central a role in the compositions of the next generation. Thus these pieces place none of the demands on the performer that would call for the extensive use of the thumb as a pivot finger.

Retention of Earlier Fingering Practices

If Emanuel Bach's ideas are indeed those of his father, then why does Emanuel not explain the principles evident both in his father's fingerings and in the other decisive secondary sources? The answer to this question is, of course, that he does explain them; he mentions them often, and demands that they be mastered in the same way as the use of the thumb:

Die Abwechselung der Finger ist der hauptsächlichste Vorwurff der Applicatur. Wir können mit unsern fünf Fingern nur fünf Töne nach einander anschlagen; folglich mercke man vornehmlich zwey Mittel, wodurch wir bequem so viel Finger gleichsam kriegen als wir brauchen. Diese zwey Mittel bestehen in dem Untersetzen und Ueberschlagen.

Da die Natur keinen von allen Fingern so geschickt gemacht hat, sich unter die übrigen andere so zu biegen, als den Daumen, so beschäftiget sich dessen Biegsamkeit samt seiner vortheilhaften Kürtze gantz allein mit dem Untersetzen an den Oertern und zu der Zeit, wenn die Finger nicht hinreichen wollen.

Das Ueberschlagen geschiehet von den andern Fingern und wird dadurch erleichtert, indem ein grösserer Finger über einen kleinern oder den Daumen geschlagen wird, wenn es gleichfals an Fingern fehlen will. Dieses Ueberschlagen muss durch die Uebung auf eine geschickte Art ohne Verschränckung geschehen.

Change of fingers is the most important element of fingering. Our five fingers can strike only five successive tones, but there are two principal means whereby we can comfortably gain as many fingers as we need. These are the turning of the thumb (das Untersetzen) and the crossing of the fingers (das Ueberschlagen).

Since nature has endowed no other finger with the skill to pass under the others, the thumb uses its flexibility, together with its advantageous shortness, to turn under at places and times when there are not sufficient fingers to execute a passage.

Crossing over is a technique limited to the remaining fingers, and is made easier when a longer finger vaults a shorter, including the thumb, when there are not enough fingers to execute a passage. This crossing must be practiced until the fingers are skillful enough not to interlock.—*Versuch*, p. 23 (Mitchell, pp. 45—46).

While modern performers are inclined to view the crossing of fingers other than the thumb as unusual and awkward, Emanuel Bach views it as a common aspect of the crossing of fingers. He states earlier in the chapter that both the crossing of the fingers and the turning of the thumb are indispensable (see quote, p. 17 above).

In the scale fingerings provided in the *Versuch*, Emanuel Bach manifestly retains the use of earlier fingering patterns. The scale for C major ascending,[26] for example, is furnished with three alternate fingering patterns for each hand, among which we find the following:

The third application of these fingerings[27] is as follows:

Furthermore, Bach informs us that these patterns are the more common ones (although the normal modern fingering for a C major scale he also considers common):

Keine davon ist verwerflich, ohngeachtet die mit dem Ueberschlagen des dritten Fingers über den vierten in der rechten Hand und in der lincken des zweyten Fingers über den Daumen, und die allwo der Daumen in F wieder eingesetzt wird, vielleicht gewöhnlicher seyn mögen als die dritte Art.

None of them [i. e., the fingering patterns for C major ascending] is objectionable, although those in which the third finger of the right hand crosses the fourth, the second of the left hand crosses the thumb, and the one in which the thumb is brought in upon F [i. e., r. h. 1231234...] are perhaps more usual than the third way.—*Versuch*, p. 24 (Mitchell, pp. 46—47).

Later in the chapter he tells why these fingerings are more usual:

Deswegen ist in den Ton-Arten mit keinen oder wenigen Versetzungs-Zeichen bey gewissen Fällen das

---

[26]Tab. I., Fig. I (Mitchell, p. 46).
[27]Tab. I., Fig. II (Mitchell, p. 47).

Ueberschlagen des dritten Fingers über den vierten und des zweiten über den Daumen besser und nützlicher, um alles mögliche Absetzen zu vermeiden, als der übrige Gebrauch des Ueberschlagens und das Untersetzen des Daums, weil selbiger bey vorkommenden halben Tönen mehr Platz und folglich auch mehr Bequemlichkeit hat, unter die anderen Finger durchzukriechen, als bey einer Folge von lauter unten liegenden Tasten. Bey den Ton-Arten ohne Versetzungs-Zeichen geschiehet dieses Ueberschlagen ohne Gefahr des Stolperns hinter einander; bey den andern aber muss man wegen der halben Töne mehr Behutsamkeit brauchen.

In keys with few or no accidentals the crossing of the third finger over the fourth and the second over the thumb is in certain cases better and more useful in attaining unbroken continuity than the excessive use of crossing or the turning of the thumb. With regard to the latter [i. e., the turning under of the thumb], when a black key acts as the pivot the thumb is provided with more room and consequently more ease in which to pass under the other fingers than in a succession of white keys. In keys without accidentals this crossing should happen without danger of stumbling, but in the others one must exercise more care because of the black keys.—*Versuch*, p. 35 (Mitchell, p. 58).

The scales of C major descending, A minor descending, and G major, F major, D minor, G minor, and D major ascending are also provided with one pattern (among others) in which the third finger crosses the fourth (in the right and left hands) and the second crosses the thumb (again in both the right and left hands). These patterns, then, are derived from principles of earlier fingering that were transmitted to Emanuel Bach from his father.

It should not be a cause for surprise that the earlier fingering patterns which Emanuel records are not precisely those of his father (as seen, for example, in the *Applicatio*). It seems probable that what J. S. Bach transmitted to his students was not a precise set of early fingerings, one invariable pattern for each scale, but rather a general method or procedure in the use of finger crossings, which Emanuel Bach then applied in the construction of the specific scale patterns in the *Versuch*. Consistent with his statement of principles, Emanuel Bach begins to restrict scale fingering patterns to the turning under of the thumb as soon as an increase in the number of accidentals occurs.

In addition to his explanation of finger crossings, Emanuel Bach also mentions the use of the same finger on two notes in succession:

Da der Daumen von unsern Vorfahren nur selten gebraucht wurde, so war er ihnen oft im Wege; folglich hatten sie manchmahl zu viel Finger. Als man nachhero solchen fleissiger zu gebrauchen anfing, so mengte sich die alte Art noch oft unter die neue und man hatte gleichsam noch nicht das Herz, den Daumen allezeit da, wo er hingehöret, einzusetzen. Jetzo empfinden wir dann und wann, ohngeachtet des bessern Gebrauchs der Finger bey unserer Art von Musick, dass wir deren zu wenig haben.

Dahero muss man zu weilen erlauben mit einem Finger, auch bey gehenden Noten, fortzugehen. Am öftersten und leichtesten geschiehet dieses, wenn man wegen der Folge von einem halben Tone in die nächste Taste mit dem Finger herunter gleitet.... Da dieses Herabgleiten sehr leichte fält, so kan es auch ausser dieser Ursache und in geschwinderer Zeit-Masse gebraucht werden als das Fortsetzen und Ablösen. Uebrigens mercke man besonders hierbey an, dass das Fortsetzen in gewissen Fällen eben so geschickt ist, gestossene Noten heraus zu bringen als geschleiffte.

Because our forerunners rarely used the thumb, it often got in the way. Hence, they had at times too many fingers. When it later began to be used more freely, the old method was often still mixed in with the new, and players were not always of a mind to use the thumb where it belonged. Today, despite the better use of our fingers in our style of music, we feel now and then that we have too few of them.

Because of this, it is at times permissible to use a finger twice in succession even when the notes change. This occurs most frequently and naturally in moving from a black key to an adjacent white one.... Since this slide downward is so simple, it may be employed for other purposes, too, and in faster tempos than those suitable for substitution and finger repetition on a single tone. Observe that it may be used to perform detached as well as slurred notes.—*Versuch*, pp. 45—46 (Mitchell, p. 73).

This rather sparse advice can be augmented and clarified by examples to be found in the *Versuch* and in the *Probestücke* (pieces that Emanuel wrote to illustrate his principles as stated in the *Versuch*):

C. P. E. Bach, *Sechs Sonaten: Achtzehn Probestücke zu dem "Versuch über die wahre Art das Clavier zu spielen"* (1753), ed. Erich Doflein (Mainz: B. Schott's Söhne, 1935), Vol. I, p. 8, mm. 21—22 (left hand) and p. 10, mm. 4—5 (right hand).

Examples such as these are not frequent in the *Probestücke*, however, in part because the pieces are not copiously fingered, in part because their textures are sparse and homophonic and thus have no need of the device.

Interdependence of Fingering and Style

J. S. Bach's cultivation of the use of the thumb, then, which was the most novel aspect of his all-embracing technique, was adopted by his students as the major feature of their fingering technique. Decisive in this change is the development of the new style that, with its frequent scale passages and rests and its sparse textures in conjunction with the increasing use of accidentals, made the change preeminently practical. C. P. E. Bach says this at the outset of his chapter on fingering:

Unsere Vorfahren, welche sich überhaupt mehr mit der Harmonie als Melodie abgaben, spielten folglich auch meistentheils vollstimmig. Wir werden aus der Folge ersehen, dass bey dergleichen Gedancken, indem man sie meistentheils nur auf eine Art heraus bringen kan, und sie nicht so gar viel Veränderungen haben, jedem Finger seine Stelle gleichsam angewiesen ist; folglich sind sie nicht so verführerisch wie die melodischen Passagien, weil der Gebrauch der Finger bey diesen letztern viel willkührlicher ist, als bey jenen. Vor diesem war das Clavier nicht so gut temperirt wie heut zu Tage, folglich brauchte man nicht alle vier und zwanzig Tonarten wie anjetzo und man hatte also auch nicht die Verschiedenheit von Passagien.

Our forefathers, who were more concern-ed with harmony [i. e., counterpoint] than melody [i. e., homophony], consequently played in several parts most of the time. We can see as a consequence that in this style [i. e., a contrapuntal one] the position of each finger is immediately apparent since most passages can be expressed in only one way and are variable to only a limited degree. Consequently, they are not so treacherous as melodic passages with their far more capricious fingering. Formerly keyboard instruments were not so well tempered as nowadays, and thus all twenty-four keys were not used as they are now; therefore there was not such a great variety of passages.—*Versuch*, pp. 16—17 (Mitchell, p. 42).

Kirnberger's *Clavierübungen mit der Bachischen Applicatur* is perhaps the most striking proof that the change in style was decisive in the change in fingering techniques. All of the pieces in this publication (save one) are in the then-fashionable galant style: dances and other lighter pieces with sparse textures, arpeggiated figures, frequent rests and scale passages. These pieces are all fingered according to the principles set forth in C. P. E. Bach's *Versuch*. The one exception is the "Allabreve" (Pachelbel's Magnificat fugue), in the older contrapuntal style, which Kirnberger has fingered in a thoroughly different manner—a manner in every way analogous to the fingering in BWV 870a (also contrapuntal in texture, but fingered some 30 years earlier).

If the style change is decisive in fingering practice, then the change in attitude and outlook that accompanied it is even more so. J. S. Bach, whose outlook belonged essentially to an age (or ages) past, was chiefly concerned with perfecting his art (both performance and composition) and teaching it. The systematization of the details of his performance technique was apparently of lesser interest to him. His speculative bent seems to have been directed primarily toward the exploration of new musical territory (e. g., the use of all 24 keys and the interpenetration of styles) and the cosmic aspect of musical expression (e. g., the mystical significance of number in music, the heritage of the Middle Ages).

C. P. E. Bach, on the other hand, was a child of the Enlightenment, one of whose cardinal tenets was the notion that all things must be ordered and reasonable. This notion lies behind the comprehensive, reasonable, and orderly *Versuch*; it also underlies the consistent use of thumb-under fingering, which can be reduced to a few simple and broadly applicable principles (in contrast to the complex and situation-bound yet eminently practical combination of early and more modern modes of fingering that J. S. Bach employed to perform his densely contrapuntal works).

This essential difference in outlook explains whatever inconsistencies exist between statements of C. P. E. Bach and the fingering found in the other sources. Emanuel Bach limits the crossing of fingers to 3 over 4 (besides, of course, other fingers crossing the thumb);[28] the other sources exhibit a far greater variety of finger crossings. Emanuel Bach makes only cursory mention of using the same finger on two notes in succession; this practice is abundantly evident in the other sources. In fact, Emanuel Bach's attitude toward the vestiges of earlier fingering (which he himself used and supported) seems to be one of mild embarrassment. It is almost as if he assumes an apologetic tone when he briefly discusses them, since they are not reasonable, not systematic, but rather practical. He treats them rather like a bit of dust in an otherwise immaculate room, to be quickly swept under the carpet as soon as it is noticed.

The Demise of Early Fingerings

C. P. E. Bach's use of these fingerings is, of course, an inconsistency in itself; 343434 and 121212 are glaring contradictions to the neat rules of thumb-under fingering. Keyboard performers of the next generation, even those directly in the Bach tradition (i.e., grandpupils), were quick to correct his "mistakes." In 1789 (one year after Emanuel's death) Johann Carl Friedrich Rellstab, a student of J. F. Agricola and an ardent admirer of C. P. E. Bach, published an edition of C. P. E. Bach's *Probestücke*, prefaced by his own brief *Anleitung* (based heavily on the *Versuch*). In his chapter on fingering he reproduces Bach's patterns and applications for the C major scale

[28] *Versuch*, Tab. I, Fig. I & p. 33 (Mitchell, pp. 46 & 57).

ascending, but he adds fingering to the third application in this manner:

Hr. C. Bach glaubt, dass die in der rechten Hand, wo der dritte Finger über dem vierten, und jene in der linken Hand, wo der zweite über dem Daumen schlägt, die gewöhnlichen sind, aber gewiss wenig Clavierspieler sind dabey mit ihm gleicher Meynung. Die Applicatur mit dem Ueberschlagen des dritten Fingers über dem vierten, so wie des vierten über den fünften, glaube ich, schreibt sich noch von der Zeit her, wo man den Daumen gar nicht brauchte, und werden gewiss die meisten Clavierspieler das dritte Beyspiel mit der von mir darüber gesetzten mit grössern Ziffern gedruckten Applicatur bequemer finden. Auch kann hierbey der Anschlag nie kräftig werden, da der Finger auf der Mitte der Taste, der Länge nach, und nie vorne zu liegen kommt. Im Anfangsstück, Pag. 28, No. 43, ist diese Applicatur angebracht. Zwey geschickte Clavierspieler, die die Correctur mit mir besorgten, schrieben darüber: Diese Fingersetzung ist mir auffallend; ich würde, in dem Laufe h anstatt des dritten Fingers lieber den ersten untergesetzt haben, und dies ist meine Meynung auch. Bey dem einzigen Fall, wo ein einzelner falsch sogenannter halber Ton, eine Passagie schliest, halte ich es für bequemer, den längern Finger über den kürzern zu schlagen. Z. B.

Sonst muss ich gestehen, ist sie mir durchgängig unbequem; und ich überlasse es daher den Einsichten der Claviermeister, in wiefern sie sie bey ihren Schülern brauchen wollen.

Bey C dur im Absteigen, gilt meist was ich oben im Aufsteigen gesagt habe.

Mr. C. Bach believes that the one [i. e., scale fingering] for the right hand in which the third finger strikes over the fourth, and the one for the lower hand in which the second finger strikes over the thumb, are the most common, but very few keyboard players hold the same opinion as he does. The fingering with the crossing of the third finger over the fourth, as well as the fourth finger over the fifth, I believe, comes down to us from the time when one did not use the thumb; certainly most keyboard players will find the third application to be more comfortable when performed with the fingering that I have placed above it printed in larger figures [i. e., using the thumb as a pivot]. With this method, also, the attack can never be solid, since the finger comes to rest upon the middle of the key [longways], and not on its forward edge. In the *Anfangsstück* [i. e., *Probestück*], p. 28, No. 43, this fingering [i. e., the earlier type] has been used. Two accomplished keyboard players who helped me with proofreading wrote over it: This fingering is surprising to me; in performing the b-natural I would rather have brought the thumb under instead of using the third finger. This is also my opinion. Only in the situation where a single half-step ending on an accidental closes a run do I suggest it would be more comfortable to pass the longer finger over the shorter. For example:

(See example on previous page.)

Otherwise I must insist that it is quite uncomfortable for me; I shall therefore leave the matter to the discretion of keyboard teachers, to what extent they wish to use it with their students.

In C major descending what I have said above about the ascending scale also holds true.—Johann Carl Friedrich Rellstab, *C. P. E. Bachs Anfangsstücke mit einer Anleitung den Gebrauch dieser Stücke, die Bachsche Fingersetzung, die Manieren und den Vortrag betreffend* (Berlin: Verlage der Rellstabschen Musikhandlung... 1789), p. IV.

Daniel Gottlob Türk and August Eberhard Müller, both grandpupils of J. S. Bach, give nothing but modern, thumb-under fingerings for all scales.[29] Both also forbid the use of the same finger on two notes in succession, since it breaks the legato line, and both discourage vaulting one finger with another, except in moving from a natural to an accidental.[30]

The closing word in the chapter on early fingering is spoken by Wolfgang Amadeus Mozart (who, of course, was not in the direct lineage of Bach's pupils), who in a letter to his father (Jan. 17, 1778) castigates a keyboard performer because, among other defects, "he executes all descending runs in the right hand with the first finger and thumb."[31]

[29]D. G. Türk, *Kleines Lehrbuch für Anfänger im Klavierspielen* (Halle u. Leipzig: Schwickert, 1802), pp. 56 ff.; A. E. Müller, *Forte-piano-Schule* (Leipzig: C. F. Peters, [1804]), pp. 37 ff.

[30]Türk, *Kleines Lehrbuch*, pp. 54—55; Müller, p. 34.

[31]From a partial translation in: Carol MacClintock, ed., *Readings in the History of Music in Performance* (Bloomington & London: Indiana University Press, [c. 1979]), p. 383.

Articulation

In discussing articulation it is again necessary to draw the distinction between, on the one hand, the aurally perceived effect of phrasing at any given moment in performance (i.e., that which arises from the performer's interpretation of the peculiar melodic, harmonic, and textural demands at any point in the score) and, on the other, the basic presuppositions regarding proper articulation that have been held by performers in general in any given period or school. The former must always remain in large measure a matter of conjecture as subsequent ages attempt to recreate it. Concerning the latter, however, there is extant evidence from contemporary sources that we may examine in order to form a general impression of opinion and practice.

A. ORDINARY ARTICULATION

There are a number of 18th-century writers, some of whom were admirers of J. S. Bach, who describe a type of articulation that is neither legato (in the modern sense of the word) nor clearly detached, and that they present as being the normal type of articulation employed in keyboard performance:

Weil aber dieses Auf- und Nieder-Gehen mit den Fingern seine geweisete Wege hat, kann folgende Vorschrifft dabey zu Rathe gezogen werden. Man setzt den Mittel-Finger der lincken Hand auf das C, und drückt es sanffte nieder; den Zeige-Finger hernach, wenn jener wieder aufgehoben worden, auf das D; den Daumen, nach aufgehobenem Zeige-Finger auf das E, und wechselt so mit dem Zeige-Finger und Daumen immer ab, bis in das C....

Since however this rise and fall of the fingers has its own peculiar method, the following instruction can be adduced. One places the middle finger of the left hand upon C, and gently depresses it; then, following it, the index finger upon D, as soon as the former has been released; the thumb upon the E, after the index finger has been released, and thus continues to exchange the index finger and thumb until C has been reached....—Johann Mattheson, *Kleine general-bass-schule* (Hamburg, 1735), p. 72.

Sowohl dem Schleifen als Abstossen ist das ordentliche Fortgehen entgegen gesetzt, welches darinnen besteht, dass man ganz hurtig kurz vorher, ehe man die folgende Note berühret, den Finger von der vorhergehenden Taste aufhebet. Dieses ordentliche Fortgehen wird, weil es allezeit vorausgesetzt wird, niemahls angezeiget.

Opposed to the legato as well as the staccato is the ordinary procedure, in which one releases the finger from the previous key an instant before one plays the note following. This ordinary procedure, since it is always assumed, is never indicated.—Friedrich Wilhelm Marpurg, *Anleitung zum Clavierspielen*, second ed. (Berlin: Haude und Spener, 1765), p. 29.

Bey den Tönen, welche auf die gewöhnliche Art, d. h. weder gestossen noch geschleift, vorgetragen werden sollen, hebt man den Finger ein wenig früher, als es die Dauer der Note erfordert, von den Tasten.

In the case of tones that are to be performed in the ordinary manner, that is, neither detached nor slurred, one lifts the finger from the keys a bit earlier than the duration of the note requires.—Daniel Gottlob Türk, *Klavierschule* (1789), p. 356.

C. P. E. Bach, although he is not as specific in this regard, seems also to subscribe to the notion of an "ordinary" articulation:[32]

Einige Personen spielen kleberich, als wenn sie Leim zwischen den Fingern hätten. Ihr Anschlag ist zu lang, indem sie die Noten über die Zeit liegen lassen. Andere haben es verbessern wollen, und spielen zu kurtz; als wenn die Tasten glühend wären. Es thut aber auch schlecht. Die Mittelstrasse ist die beste; ich rede hievon überhaupt; alle Arten des Anschlages sind zur rechten Zeit gut.

Some persons play stickily, as if they had glue between their fingers. Their touch is lethargic; they hold notes too long. Others, in an attempt to correct this, play too short, as if the keys burned. Both are wrong. Midway between these extremes is best. Here again I speak in general; every kind of touch is good when used at the proper time.—*Versuch*, p. 118 (Mitchell, p. 149).

The fingering found in the sources already examined also suggests a mode of playing that is somewhat more detached than modern legato. The frequent use of the same finger on two notes in succession, the avoidance of substitution, the crossing and unusual leaps of fingers—none of these can be employed if the articulation is to be totally legato. Furthermore, if we are to believe that Bach's touch at the keyboard was characterized by an "uninterrupted evenness" (see next page), then the above practices must have been integrated into the touch in such a way that they were not obtrusive. A touch somewhat more articulate than modern legato is thus a logical result of these fingerings.

Emanuel Bach's compositional style is manifestly not that of his father, and it is therefore well advised, when attempting to understand his father's ideas through the *Versuch*, to be more cautious in accepting statements on performance practice than on keyboard technique. The following remarks should indeed be considered, though to what degree they apply to J. S. Bach's practice must remain moot:

Die Lebhaftigkeit des Allegro wird gemeiniglich in gestossenen Noten und das Zärtliche des Adagio in getragenen und geschleiften Noten vorgestellet. Man hat also beym Vortrage darauf zu sehen, dass diese Art und Eigenschaft des Allegro und Adagio in Obacht genommen werde, wenn auch dieses bey den Stücken nicht angedeutet ist, und der Spieler noch nicht hinlängliche Einsichten in den Affekt eines Stückes hat. Ich setze oben mit Fleiss gemeiniglich, weil ich wohl weiss, dass allerhand Arten von Noten bey allerhand Arten der Zeitmaasse vorkommen können.

...Ueberhaupt kan man sagen dass das Stossen mehrentheils bey springenden Noten und in geschwinder Zeitmaasse vorkommt.

...Ueberhaupt zu sagen, so kommen die Schleiffungen mehrentheils bey gehenden Noten und in langsamer oder gemässigter Zeit-Maasse vor.

In general the briskness of allegros is expressed by detached notes and the tenderness of adagios by grave, slurred notes. The performer must keep in mind that these characteristic features of allegros and adagios are to be taken into consideration even when a composition is not so marked, as well as when the performer has not yet gained an adequate understanding of the effect of a piece. I use the expression "in general" advisedly, for I am well aware that all kinds of execution may appear in any tempo.

...Generally speaking, detached notes appear mostly in leaping passages and rapid tempos.

---

[32]C. P. E. Bach makes this curious statement in the *Versuch*:

Die Noten, welche weder gestossen noch geschleifft noch ausgehalten werden, unterhält man so lange als ihre Hälffte beträgt; es sey denn, dass das Wörtlein Ten. (gehalten) darüber steht, in welchem Falle man sie aushalten muss. Diese Art Noten sind gemeiniglich die Achttheile und Viertheile in gemässigter und langsamer Zeit-Maasse.... Tones which are neither detached, slurred nor fully held are sustained for half their value, unless the abbreviation "Ten." (hold) is written over them, in which case they must be held fully. Quarters and eighths in moderate and slow tempos are usually performed in this manner....—P. 127 (Mitchell, p. 157).

In addition to seemingly contradicting other statements by Emanuel Bach, this opinion is carefully and thoughtfully opposed by Daniel Gottlob Türk (a grandpupil of J. S. Bach):

Bach sagt...: "Die Noten, welche weder gestossen noch geschleift noch ausgehalten werden, unterhält man so lange als ihre Hälfte beträgt etc." Allein im Ganzen genommen scheint mir diese Spielart doch nicht die beste zu seyn. Denn 1) macht der Charakter eines Tonstückes hierbey verschiedene Einschränkungen nothwendig; 2) würde dadurch der Unterschied zwischen den wirklich abzustossenden und nur auf die gewöhnliche Art zu spielenden Noten beynahe ganz aufgehoben; 3) möchte der Vortrag doch wohl zu kurz (hackend) werden, wenn man jeden nicht zu schleifenden etc. Ton nur die Hälfte seiner Dauer aushielte, und folglich die zweyte Hälfte pausirte....

[C. P. E.] Bach says...: "Tones that are neither detached, slurred nor fully held are sustained for half their value, etc." On the whole, however, this type of performance seems to me to be not the best. For 1) a piece's character itself imposes various restrictions [i. e., a uniform style of performance would be boring]; 2) the difference between the truly detached notes and those only to be played in the ordinary manner would thereby almost entirely be erased; 3) the performance might indeed become too short (choppy), if one held every unconnected...note for only half its value, and then rested for the second half....—D. G. Türk, *Klavierschule*, p. 356.

...Generally speaking, slurred notes appear mostly in stepwise passages and in slower or more moderate tempos.— *Versuch*, pp. 118, 125, & 126 (Mitchell, pp. 149, 154, & 155).

In contrast to the evidence implying a slightly detached manner of performance are a number of statements supporting the impression of smoothness and connection of tones that Bach's performance gave. J. S. Bach himself never mentions articulation in any of his extant writings, yet in his recommendation on the title page of the *Inventions* (1723) he does advocate the development of a "cantabile" manner of performance:

Auffrichtige Anleitung, wormit denen Liebhabern des Claviers, besonders aber denen Lehrbegierigen, eine deutliche Art gezeiget wird...am allermeisten aber eine cantabile Art im Spielen zu erlangen....

Upright instruction wherein the lovers of the keyboard, and especially those desirous of learning, are shown a clear way . . . above all to arrive at a singing style of playing.... —*Bach Reader*, p. 86.

This cantabile manner Emanuel Bach also prizes:

Der gute Vortrag ist also sofort daran zu erkennen, wenn man alle Noten nebst den ihnen zugemessenen guten Manieren zu rechter Zeit in ihrer gehörigen Stärcke durch einen nach dem wahren Inhalte des Stücks abgewognen Druck mit einer Leichtigkeit hören lässt. Hieraus entstehet das Runde, Reine und Fliessende in der Spielart, und wird man dadurch deutlich und ausdrückend.

Good performance, then, may immediately be recognized when one hears all notes with their proper embellishments played with ease in correct time with fitting volume produced by a touch which is related to the true content of a piece. Herein lies the rounded, pure, flowing manner of playing that creates clarity and expressiveness.—*Versuch*, p. 117 (Mitchell, p. 148).

and he cautions:

Das Untersetzen und Ueberschlagen als die Haupt-Hülffs-Mittel in der Abwechselung der Finger müssen so gebraucht werden, dass alle Töne dadurch gut zusammen gehänget werden können.

Turning and crossing, the principal means of changing the fingers, must be used in such a manner that all the tones can thereby be well connected.—*Versuch*, pp. 34—35 (Mitchell, p. 58).

J. S. Bach's friend and defender Johann Abraham Birnbaum remarks on the smoothness of Bach's touch at the keyboard:

...die gantz besondere geschicklichkeit auch bey der grösten geschwindigkeit, alle Thöne deutlich und mit durchgängiger gleichheit auszudrücken....

...the quite special adroitness, even at the greatest speed, in bringing out all the tones clearly and with uninterrupted evenness....—J. A. Birnbaum, "Impartial comments on a questionable passage in the sixth number of 'Der critische Musicus,' " 1738 (*Bach-Dokumente 2*, p. 300; *Bach Reader*, p. 242).

Finally, Ernst Ludwig Gerber, a grandpupil of Bach, in his *Tonkünstler-Lexicon* (1790—92) says of the organist Schröter:

Wer aber die vortrefliche gebundene Manier kennt, mit welcher Sebastian Bach die Orgel behandelte, dem konnte Schröters Manier unmöglich gefallen, indem er seine Orgel durchaus staccato traktirte.

Schröter's manner could not possibly please those who knew Bach's excellent legato manner of organ playing, for he played everything on the organ staccato.—*Bach-Dokumente 3*, p. 473 (*Bach Reader*, p. 186 n.).

Whatever type of touch J. S. Bach employed, it is clear that his keyboard performance gave the aural impression of a singing legato style.

In this regard it is also important to consider the nature of the mechanical action of the organs upon which Bach performed. Keys were not held up by springs under them, but were connected by trackers to the pallets under each pipe channel; the spring under the pallet, then, not only held the pallet firmly closed, but it also held the key up. When any of the keys was depressed, its pallet reacted instantaneously by beginning to open; likewise, the pallet did not fully close until the key had risen completely. On this type of action a pipe continues to speak from the first instant a key is depressed until the moment the finger ceases to be in contact with the key (compare this with the piano, whose attack point is at the bottom of the key, or the electro-pneumatic pipe organ, whose attack and release points are usually at some point midway in the key's course of travel). What all this means for articulation is best understood by firsthand experience on early organ keyboards. Briefly stated, it is possible to achieve a more legato effect with early fingering practices on such a keyboard than on any keyboard with a more modern type of action.

Finally, Bach's quiet keyboard technique has to be taken into account, and more especially his method of releasing a note. When a given finger is drawn backwards on a key, it then moves slightly behind the other fingers. Any other finger that crosses it, then, can do so more readily and rapidly, since the first finger has been drawn out of the way. This sort of release allows finger crossings to be executed in a much more connected manner than is possible when all the fingertips remain at the same point along the length of the keys.

These, then, are the elements that must be taken into account and balanced in trying to determine the type of touch that is basic to Bach's keyboard technique:

More Detached
1. the "ordinary" type of keyboard articulation prevalent during and after Bach's lifetime;
2. the evidence provided by fingerings in the primary and secondary sources;
3. statements by C. P. E. Bach on the appropriate circumstances for detached and slurred performance.

More Connected
1. the cantabile impression that Bach's keyboard performance gave;
2. the peculiar characteristics of key action in the organs Bach played;
3. Bach's quiet technique and his method of releasing keys.

In evaluating these elements it needs to be said that they need not be viewed as being contradictory. Experimentation with the "ordinary" type of articulation will reveal that it can create the impression of a cantabile manner of performance just as well as the modern legato touch. Fidelity to all aspects of Bach's technique as we know it will go a long way toward automatically producing the basic articulation proper to his music.

E. L. Gerber's remark in his *Tonkünstler-Lexicon* (previous page) needs to be understood in light of the then-prevailing taste for a more detached manner of keyboard performance. This taste was peculiar to the second half of the 18th century and stands in marked contrast to the preferences of those eras both preceding and following it:

Bey einem schweren Vortrage muss nämlich jeder Ton fest (nachdrücklich) angegeben und bis zur völlig verflossenen Dauer der Noten ausgehalten werden. Leicht heisst also der Vortrag, wenn man jeden Ton mit weniger Festigkeit (Nachdruck) angiebt, und den Finger etwas früher, als es die Dauer der Noten bestimmt, von den Tasten abhebt. Zur Vermeidung eines Missverständnisses muss ich hierbey noch anmerken, dass sich die Ausdrücke schwer und leicht überhaupt mehr auf das Aushalten und Absetzen der Töne, als auf die Stärke und Schwäche derselben beziehen. Denn in Gewissen Fällen z.B. in einem Allegro vivo, scherzando, Vivace con allegrezza &c. muss zwar der Vortrag ziemlich leicht (kurz), aber dabey doch mehr oder weniger stark seyn; da hingegen ein Tonstück von traurigem Charakter z.B. ein Adagio mesto, con afflizzione &c. zwar geschleift und folglich gewissermassen schwer, dessen ungeachtet aber nicht eben stark vorgetragen werden darf....

Eben so setzt auch die Manier des Komponisten eine eigene Behandlungsart voraus. Ein Tonstück von Händel, Sebastian Bach &c. muss nachdrücklicher vorgetragen werden, als etwa ein modernes Konzert von Mozart, Kozeluch u. a. m.

In a heavy [sustained] performance each tone must be rendered emphatically (nachdrücklich) and held out through the entire duration of the note. A light performance is characterized by rendering each note with less firmness (emphasis), and lifting the finger from the keys somewhat earlier than the duration of the notes specifies. In order to avoid misunderstanding I must note in this regard that the expressions *heavy* and *light* refer in general more to the duration and release of the notes than to their strength or weakness [i. e., in dynamic level]. For in specific instances, e. g. in an Allegro vivo, scherzando, Vivace con allegrezza, etc., the performance must indeed be light (short), yet at the same time more or less strong; by the same token a composition of a sad character, e.g., an Adagio mesto, con afflizzione, etc., must indeed be slurred and in consequence relatively grave, regardless of whether or not it is to be performed strongly....

The style of a composer presupposes a particular type of treatment. A composition by Handel, Sebastian Bach, etc., must be played more emphatically than a modern concerto by

Mozart, Kozeluch, and others like them.—Daniel Gottlob Türk, *Klavierschule*, pp. 358—59 & 364.

Hierauf ging er mit mir die zu diesem Lehrbuch gehörigen Übungstücke durch und machte mich vorzüglich auf das Legato aufmerksam, das er selber in einer so unübertrefflichen Art in seiner Macht hatte, und das zu jener Zeit alle andern Pianisten auf dem Forte-piano für unausführbar hielten, indem damals (noch von Mozarts Zeit) das gehackte und kurz abgestossene Spiel Mode war. Auch hat mir in späteren Jahren Beethoven erzählt, dass er Mozart mehrmal spielen gehört und dass dieser, da zu seiner Zeit die Erfindung der Fortepiano noch in ihrer Kindheit war, sich auf den damals mehr gebräuchlichen Flügeln ein Spiel angewohnt hatte, welches keineswegs für die Fortepiano passte. Auch hatte ich in der Folge die Bekanntschaft mehrerer Personen gemacht, welche bei Mozart Unterricht genommen, und fand in ihrer Spielweise diese Bemerkung bestätigt.

He [Beethoven] then had me play through the studies given in the manual [i. e., C. P. E. Bach's *Versuch*] and pointed out especially the legato, which he himself had mastered to such an incomparable degree, and which all other pianists of that time considered to be impossible to execute on the fortepiano, as it was still the fashion (as in Mozart's time) to play in a detached, abrupt manner. Beethoven himself told me in later years that he had heard Mozart play on several occasions, and that Mozart had developed a mode of playing on the claviers of that time that was not at all suitable to the forte-piano. Some years later I also made the acquaintance of several persons who had studied under Mozart, and found Beethoven's remark borne out by their playing.—Carl Czerny, *Erinnerungen aus meinem Leben* (1842), ed. & annotated by W. Kolneder (Strasbourg & Baden-Baden: Heitz, 1968), p. 15; trans. in Carol MacClintock, ed., *Readings in the History of Music in Performance* (Bloomington & London: Indiana University Press, [c. 1979], p. 384).

B. ARTICULATION AND METER

The concept of articulation held universally among keyboard performers through the first years of the 18th century involved the grouping of notes not according to phrases, but according to their place in the metrical structure. Notes that occurred on the beat received greater regard and stress than those off the beat. In other words: Though the motive or phrase might be the determining factor in the compositional process (and might even sit astride two or more beats), the meter was the determining factor in articulation. In numerous treatises of the time this concept is referred to as *quantitas intrinseca*, "superior regard," "good and bad" notes, "struck and passing" notes, "intrinsically long and short" notes, and "heavy and light" notes.[33]

In keyboard performance this grouping was not merely theoretical but was also translated into an aurally perceptible organization of the measure in such a way that notes on the beat were stressed by slightly more prominent articulations before their attack. Thus a bar line indicated not merely a theoretical metrical division but probably marked the location of the most prominent articulation in the measure, i. e., before the first and strongest beat.

This is most clearly visible in the early fingering patterns previously discussed (pp. 21—22 above). These fingerings arise not from motives or phrases (i. e., compositional units) but from the mechanically repetitive pattern of accents established by the meter. For example, in the pattern 343434 the third finger is normally placed on a metrically stressed note (a note on a beat). In the alternation of third and fourth fingers the third finger must repeatedly vault the fourth in order to attack the following note. Even taking into account the "ordinary" type of articulation (see pp. 39—40 above), this vaulting tends to produce a slightly more prominent articulation before the stressed note (especially in more rapid passages) and thus subtly to group the stressed note and the unstressed one following it together.

---

[33]The entire matter of note groupings during the period 1650—1800, including its involvement with articulation and with "inegal" performance, is discussed in George L. Houle's "The Musical Measure as Discussed by Theorists from 1650—1800" (unpubl. Ph.D. diss., Stanford University, 1961), pp. 173 ff. See also Jean-Claude Zehnder, "Organ Articulation in the Seventeenth and Eighteenth Centuries," Part II, *The American Organist*, Vol. 17, No. 12 (December 1983), pp. 41—43. A source that elucidates the importance of meter and its relation to tempo and performance is J. P. Kirnberger's *Die Kunst des reinen Satzes in der Musik*, Vol. II, Part I, 1776; trans. David Beach and Jurgen Thym, *The Art of Strict Musical Composition* (New Haven: Yale University Press, [1982]), pp. 381—403. After establishing the aesthetic foundations of meter, Kirnberger proceeds to treat each meter in turn, describing its structure and execution, its spirit and character. Although this source is late, it is markedly retrospective; not only does Kirnberger belong to J. S. Bach's most intimate circle, but in this book he frequently refers to pieces by earlier composers (especially J. S. Bach) to illustrate his statements.

There can be little doubt that the subtle mechanical grouping of notes was an ordinary feature of keyboard performance throughout the 17th and early 18th centuries.[34] But to what degree is it applicable to the music of J. S. Bach?

It is hardly conceivable that Bach in his youth would have known or practiced as a rule any other type of articulation than the traditional note groupings determined by metrical structure. This sort of articulation is certainly suggested by the early fingering patterns found in the *Applicatio*. One cannot automatically assume, though, that all of Bach's keyboard music should be interpreted by the imposition of earlier mechanical patterns of articulation. Indeed, although the fingerings found in his works largely reflect these patterns, there are instances where technical demands occasion fingerings that could promote exactly the opposite type of articulation.[35] More to the point, the notion of a mechanical pattern of articulation bound to the metrical structure began to weaken during the same period when keyboard performers started to experiment with more modern fingering practices, i. e., the first half of the 18th century.[36] Bach did not live in a musical vacuum. He both heard and experimented with the new arbitrary type of note grouping characteristic of preclassical, classical, and romantic music, which the composer indicates by means of slurs over groups of notes (frequently obscuring the metrical structure).[37]

The most convincing evidence that the earlier type of articulation is not only applicable to most of Bach's keyboard music, but also apt and correct, is its compositional style, a style characterized by motivic construction, late baroque motor-rhythms, and unity of *Affekt*. Here again, as in the choice of modes of fingering, it is the consideration of style that is decisive. The early preludes and fugues that clearly represent the north German style, as well as the majority of the chorale settings (e. g., those in the *Orgelbüchlein*, the natural stylistic heirs of Scheidt's *Tabulatura Nova*), are stylistically logical extensions of the compositional techniques of Bach's musical forebears; their rhythmic vitality is intensified by the traditional subtle metrical grouping of notes.

No definitive word from Bach exists to tell us when (or if) he changed his performance practices to accommodate the newer style. To an even greater degree than today, personal taste governed such artistic decisions during the first half of the 18th century. French musicians formulated rules (found in the prefaces to their music publications) about good taste and proper style in performance. The fact that such rules have not surfaced in 18th-century German sources before Quantz and C. P. E. Bach seems to suggest that a diverse musical life, open to and shaped by a number of musical influences (both foreign—Italian and French—and internal), encouraged diverse approaches to performance practices.

It is possible that Bach's approach gradually evolved toward that of the newer style. I think it more likely, however, that just as keyboard pieces with an affinity to the *galant* style (e. g., some of the dances in the suites, certain slow movements from the organ trio sonatas, or the Augmentation Canon from the *Art of Fugue*) are anomalies in Bach's *oeuvre* (seen in its totality), so is the new performance style to be considered essentially foreign to his practice. The closer a piece conforms to earlier compositional principles, the more likely its articulation and fingering are to be governed by the meter; the closer the piece is to works of the next generation, the more likely its articulation and fingering are to be governed by the musical phrase.

---

[34]Indeed, it seems to have survived far longer, for Franz Liszt in 1856 writes:

> ...Sei mir gestattet zu bemerken, dass ich das mechanische, taktmässige, zerschnittene Auf- und Abspielen, wie es an manchen Orten noch üblich ist, möglichst beseitigt wünsche, und nur den periodischen Vortrag, mit dem Hervortreten der besonderen Accente und der Abrundung der melodischen und rhythmischen Nuancirung, als sachgemäss anerkennen kann.
> ...May I be permitted to remark that I wish to avoid as far as possible that mechanical kind of playing which, meticulously adhering to the meter, splits up the performance by perpetually emphasizing the strong and weak beats, which mode of playing is, however, still customary in some places. I acknowledge only that kind of periodic style of execution which emphasizes the essential accents and displays the nuances of the music by means of melodic and rhythmic shaping.—Franz Liszt, *Sämtliche Orgelwerke*, ed. Margittay (Budapest: Editio Musica, [1970]), Vol. I, [p. II]).

[35]E. g., *Fugetta*, BWV 870a, m. 31, bass, beat 4.

[36]In this regard see Houle, pp. 219—20.

[37]An example of this arbitrary articulation in Bach's later work may be found in the Augmentation Canon in the 1751 publication of the *Art of Fugue*, the slurs in which were indisputably furnished by J. S. Bach. See "Bach's 'Art of Fugue': An Examination of the Sources," in *Current Musicology*, No. 19 (New York: Columbia University, 1975), pp. 61—64.

Pedaling

The extent of the information on Bach's keyboard technique has allowed a plausible reconstruction of his performance on the manuals. It is unfortunate that the extant information is not sufficient to allow us to form a correspondingly definitive impression of his pedaling. What follows here is, then, far more conjectural than the discussion of Bach's manual technique.

There are a number of statements in early sources that speak of Bach's phenomenal mastery of the pedals:

Mit seinen zweenen Füssen konnte er auf dem Pedale solche Sätze ausführen, die manchem nicht ungeschikten Clavieristen mit fünf Fingern zu machen sauer genug werden würden.

With his two feet he could play things on the pedals that many not unskillful clavier players would find bitter enough to have to play with five fingers.—"Nekrolog," 1754 (*Bach-Dokumente 3*, p. 88; *Bach Reader*, p. 223).

BACHIUS Lips. profundae Musices auctor his modo commemoratis non est inferior, qui, sicut HAENDELIUS apud ANGLOS, Lipsiae miraculum, quantum quidem ad Musicam attinet dici meretur, qui, si Viro placet, solo pedum ministerio, digitis aut nihil, aut aliud agentibus, tam mirificum, concitatum, celeremque in Organo ecclesiastico movet vocum concentum, ut alii digitis hoc imitari deficere videantur. Princeps sane hereditarius Hassiae FRIDERICUS

BACHIO tunc temporis, Organum, ut restitutum ad limam vocaret CASSELLAS Lipsia accersito eademque facilitate pedibus veluti alatis transtra haec, vocum gravitate reboantia, fulgurisque in morem aures praesentium terebrantia, percurrente, adeo Virum cum stupore est admiratus, ut annulum gemma distinctum, digitoque suo detractum, finito hoc musico fragore, ei dono daret. Quod munus, si pedum agilitas meruit, quid quaeso daturus fuisset Princeps...si & manus in subsidium vocasset.

Bach of Leipzig, author of profound music, is not inferior to those mentioned above [Mattheson, Keiser, Telemann]. Like Handel among the English, he deserves to be called the miracle of Leipzig, as far as music is concerned. For if it pleases him, he can by the use of his feet alone (while his fingers do either nothing or something else) achieve such an admirable, agitated, and rapid concord of sounds on the church organ that others would seem unable to imitate it even with the fingers. When he was called from Leipzig to Cassel to pronounce an organ properly restored, he ran over the pedals with this same facility, as if his feet had wings, making the organ resound with such fullness, and so penetrate the ears of those present like a thunderbolt, that Frederick, the legitimate hereditary Prince of Cassel, admired him with such astonishment that he drew a ring with a precious stone from his finger and gave it to Bach as soon as the sound had died away. If Bach earned such a gift for the agility of his feet, what, I ask, would the Prince have given him...if he had called his hands into service as well?—Constantin Bellermann, 1743 (*Bach-Dokumente 2*, p. 410; *Bach Reader*, p. 236).

Auf dem Pedale mussten seine Füsse jedes Thema, jeden Gang, ihren Vorgängern den Händen, auf das Genaueste nach machen. Kein Vorschlag, kein Mordent, kein Pralltriller durfte fehlen, oder nur weniger nett und rund zum Gehör kommen. Er machte mit beyden Füssen zugleich lange Doppeltriller, indessen die Hände nichts weniger als müssig waren.

On the pedals his feet had to imitate with perfect accuracy every theme, every passage that his hands had played. No appoggiatura, no mordent, no short trill was suffered to be lacking or even to meet the ear in less clean and rounded form. He used to make long double trills with both feet, while his hands were anything but idle.—Ernst Ludwig Gerber, *Tonkünstler-Lexicon*, 1790 (*Bach-Dokumente 3*, p. 468; *Bach Reader*, p. 263).

That Bach's skill with his feet equaled that with his hands is all the more striking when viewed in the context of pedal playing before and during his lifetime. A survey of pre-Bach organ literature in various European countries shows that the majority of works have no independent pedal part, and those works that do call for the pedal most frequently assign to it a slow-moving *cantus firmus* or a stately bass line. The exceptions to this rudimentary use of the pedal are all German, and even in that region its use was hardly consistent. Alongside works using little or no pedal there are (even at an early date) works that demand an extraordinary pedal technique. Already in the early 16th century Arnolt Schlick had written a 10-voice setting of the antiphon *Ascendo ad Patrem meum* in which four voices are assigned to the pedals, with heel and toe of the same foot playing in thirds.[38] Such virtuosic works are of course exceptional; the technique required to play them was not encountered often among organists of the time, nor was it in any way systematic.

The rise to prominence of the organ pedal division and of pedal playing took place during the 17th century in northern Germany and is first seen in the organ works of Heinrich Scheidemann (ca. 1595—1663), Matthias

Weckmann (1619—74), Franz Tunder (1614—67), Jan Adam Reinken (1623—1722), and their successors, in particular Dietrich Buxtehude (1637—1707) and Georg Böhm (1661—1733), who figure prominently in the musical formation of the young Bach. In the music of these composers the practice of alternating toes developed as the foundation of a virtuoso pedal technique.[39] In their works the role assigned to the feet gradually became equal to that assigned to the hands.[40]

The music of the north German organ school was a seminal influence upon the music of J. S. Bach, and most of the music he assigns to the pedal can be successfully executed using the techniques normative for his predecessors, namely:

1. alternating toes, either between lower and higher notes, or in short scale passages in which one toe vaults the other (analogous to early scale fingerings), and

2. the use of the same toe on two notes in succession (analogous to the use of the same finger on two notes in succession on the manuals).

But there are some pedal parts in Bach's music (especially those furnished with slurs) in which the use of the heel appears unavoidable.

There is no systematic treatment of pedal technique before Samuel Petri's *Anleitung zur praktischen Musik*,[41] followed by Daniel Gottlob Türk's *Von den wichtigsten Pflichten eines Organisten*,[42] Justin Heinrich Knecht's *Vollständige Orgelschule für Anfänger und Geübtere*,[43] and J. C. Kittel's foreword to his *Vierstimmige Choräle mit Vorspielen*.[44] All of these sources recommend the practice of two types of pedaling (in scales): one that makes use of the toes only in alternation with each

---

[38]See Willi Apel, *The History of Keyboard Music to 1700* (Bloomington & London: Indiana University Press, [1972]), pp. 89—90.

[39]See Eduard Bruggaier, "Studien zur Geschichte des Orgelpedalspiels in Deutschland bis zur Zeit Johann Sebastian Bachs" (unpubl. Ph.D. diss., Johann Wolfgang Goethe-Universität, Frankfurt am Main, Germany, 1959), pp. 55 ff. (especially p. 112).

[40]Thus Jakob Adlung in his *Musica mechanica organoedi* (Berlin: Birnstiel, 1768, Vol. II, p. 27) says:

   Die Zeiten ändern sich; jetzo will man mit den Füssen 2 bis 3 geschwänzte Noten traktieren....

   The times are changing; nowadays people want to play sixteenth and thirty-second notes with their feet....

[41]Lauban: J. C. Wirthgen, 1767 & 1782, pp. 314—31.

[42]Halle: Schwickert, 1787, pp. 158—60.

[43]Leipzig: Breitkopf und Härtel, 1795—96, pp. 43—53.

[44]Altona: J. F. Hammerich, 1803, pp. 3—4.

other,[45] and another that calls for the alternation of heel and toe of the same foot. Knecht finds the use of the heels preferable in scales to the alternation of toes (p. 47), but Kittel (a Bach pupil) calls the alternation of toes the preferable method (p. 3). Indeed, pedal playing based on the skillful use of the toes, in preference to the use of the heels, seems to have continued well into the 19th century.[46] At any rate, it seems likely that both techniques were in use well before the treatises listed above describe them in writing.

Studies undertaken to determine the normal dimensions of pedalboards during the 17th and 18th centuries, however, suggest that the use of heels was difficult at best.[47] Old pedalboards normally sloped slightly from front to back (the opposite of modern pedalboards), making it uncomfortable to reach the pedals with heels. The dimensions of Bach's still-extant Arnstadt organ console, for example, have been subjected to exhaustive measurement;[48] its high bench and short pedals (by modern standards) seem to show that in Bach's time pedalboards were still constructed to facilitate the technique of alternating toes.

Due to the lack of contemporary sources it is not possible to trace the growing role of the heel in pedal performance. It may well be that J. S. Bach, with his practical bent as well as his phenomenal pedal technique, helped to develop the use of the heel (just as he helped to develop modern fingerings). The strongest argument that his use of the heel was not well developed, however, is the ease with which the pedal lines in his music can be played by using toes almost exclusively. Perhaps this is the reason Kittel preferred to use alternating toes in scales (see above on this page): He considered it to be in most cases the most secure and dependable way to play the pedals.[49] In Bach's organ music, just as in anybody else's, pedal technique ought to conform to manual technique, and pedal touch to manual touch. In a technique that eschews substitution and seeks an articulate touch, the preference for the use of the toes in pedaling makes good sense.

---

[45]In employing this technique Türk (p. 158 n.), Knecht (pp. 43—44), and Kittel (p. 3) recommend that the left foot pass under (i. e., behind) the right, and the right over (i. e., in front of) the left. Petri (pp. 315 ff.) suggests that the left foot pass under the right in the lowest octave, and that it pass over the right above this.

[46]Even as late as 1830 Friedrich Schneider in his *Handbuch des Organisten* (Halberstadt: Carl Brüggemann, 1830), p. 63, states that one may hop or slide the toe to the neighboring pedal, and offers several examples in which the same toe hops from a natural to an accidental, glides from an accidental to a natural, and hops from an accidental to an accidental.

[47]See Jean-Claude Zehnder, "Organ Articulation in the Seventeenth and Eighteenth Centuries," Part I, *The American Organist*, Vol. 17, No. 7 (July 1983), pp. 30—31.

[48]See Ernest Zavarsky, "Zum Pedalspiel des jungen Johann Sebastian Bach," *Musikforschung*, Vol. 18 (1965), pp. 370—78, for a diagram and complete measurements of the Arnstadt console, as well as a thorough discussion of the possibilities and limitations of pedal performance the Arnstadt pedalboard afforded Bach. It should be noted, however, that Zavarsky's apparently uncritical acceptance of 19th-century articulation practices and his apparent assumption that Bach played in the modern legato manner make some of his conclusions dated. The diagram of the Arnstadt console found in Zavarsky's article is reproduced in: Sandra Soderlund, *Organ Technique: An Historical Approach* (Chapel Hill, N. C.: Hinshaw, 1980), p. 123.

---

[49]This may also be the reason Kittel calls the alternation of toe and heel the "older method"—by implication it is the less systematic, less highly developed method, a "catch as catch can" procedure that was superseded by the improved method of alternating toes. Indeed, Kittel enjoins caution in using the heel, lest the pedalboard be thereby damaged.

Conclusion

There can be no talk of understanding thoroughly Bach's keyboard style until a performer has made a serious attempt to master those elements of Bach's keyboard technique that have been handed down to us. His technique, like his music, is universal, encompassing the new as well as the old. It is truly a technique to serve all needs, and it is especially suited to the attainment of the sustained touch required for the organ. It is a technique that can deal with the technical difficulties posed by a dense contrapuntal texture, or with the demands of rapid scale passages. Its application to Bach's keyboard works not only makes them easier to perform but also enlivens their texture with myriad subtle shadings of articulation, ranging from slurring (especially at those points where Bach has expressly marked it in the score) through all the varieties of detached touch.

For the performer, mastery of this universal technique is not a matter of forgetting modern technique, but only of enlarging it by adding to it earlier fingering practices as well as those practices peculiar to J. S. Bach himself. This is best accomplished by beginning again where Bach himself must have begun—by learning pieces with fingerings from an earlier era.[50] The keyboard performer who has become conversant with these technical means will understand more fully the meaning of Philipp Spitta's extraordinary insights written a century ago:

> Thus, though his fingering is distinguished from that of his predecessors and contemporaries by the regular use of the thumb, it differs from his son's method by certain peculiarities, some of which are retained from the older method of playing, while others were naturally derived from it; the origin of Sebastian Bach's method is thus tolerably clear. It took into due consideration all the combinations which the use of the thumb now rendered possible, but without abandoning the technical accomplishment which the earlier method afforded....
>
> This combination of methods gave him such an unlimited command of means that it is easy to understand how it was that difficulties had ceased to exist for him. And, as though he had been destined in every respect to stand alone and at the summit of his art, he remained the only master of clavier-playing who acquired such stupendous technical facility. All who came before him, and all who succeeded him, worked with a much smaller supply of means; he stood on an eminence commanding two realms, and ruled that which lay before him as well as that which he had left behind.—Philipp Spitta, *Johann Sebastian Bach* (English translation, London, 1889; reprinted New York: Dover, 1951), pp. 39—40.

---

[50]In addition to the sources reproduced in this essay, such pieces may be found in:

Boxall, Maria. *Harpsichord Method*. London: Schott, [1977].

Ferguson, Howard. *Keyboard Interpretation*. New York & London: Oxford University Press, 1975. Pp. 67—79 (excerpts of pieces).

Lindley, Mark, and Maria Boxall. *Early Keyboard Fingerings: an Anthology*. London: Schott, [1982].

Rodgers, Julane. "Early Keyboard Fingering, ca. 1520—1620." Unpubl. D. M. A. diss. University of Oregon, 1971.

Soderlund, Sandra. *Organ Technique: An Historical Approach*. Chapel Hill, N. C.: Hinshaw, 1980.

Appendix I

Below is a list of early manuscript sources of Bach's works that contain fingerings, arranged so that those with the most complete fingering indications appear first. The assignment of a manuscript to a given scribe follows that given in the *Kritische Berichte* that accompany volumes in the *Neue Bach Ausgabe* and *Handschriften der Werke Johann Sebastian Bachs in der Musikbibliothek der Stadt Leipzig* (Bibliographische Veröffentlichungen der Musikbibliothek der Stadt Leipzig, 1964), as well as the analyses of handwriting that have appeared in other scholarly journals. The matter of ascription of Bach manuscript sources is only partially complete and is, of course, subject to future revision.

1. Leipzig, Musikbibliothek Ms. 7 (Sammlung Mempell-Preller), pp. 95 ff.: Canzona in D minor, BWV 588, in the hand of J. G. Preller (1727—86). Although definitely a member of Bach's circle, Preller cannot with certainty be identified as having studied directly with Bach.[51] The manuscript bears very complete fingerings that prepare the work for manuals-only performance (no notes are assigned to the pedals).

2. Leipzig, MB Ms. 7, pp. 114—15: Partita on "Sei gegrüsset," Variation I, BWV 768, hand of J. G. Preller. Numerous fingerings.

These first two sources are reproduced in APPENDIX II (pp. 131 ff.), since their complete fingerings render them of considerable interest.

3. Leipzig, MB Ms. 7, pp. 47—49: Fantasia in G minor, BWV 917, hand of J. G. Preller. Numerous fingerings.

4. Leipzig, MB Ms. 8 (Sammlung Mempell-Preller), pp. 164—65: Partita in B minor (Clavierübung II), Ouverture (appearing in this ms. in C minor), BWV 831, hand of J. G. Preller. Numerous fingerings.

5. Leipzig, MB Ms. 8, pp. 231 ff.: Fugue in A minor, BWV 944, hand of J. G. Preller. Numerous fingerings.

6. Berlin Bibliothek Mus. Ms. P595, pp. 46 ff.: Fugue in B major, BWV 955, hand of Johannes Ringk (1717—78). Partial fingering. Ringk was a pupil of J. P. Kellner, a close associate of Bach.

7. BB Mus. Ms. P803, pp. 251 ff.: Toccata in G major, BWV 916, hand of J. Wollweber. Extensive fingering. Nothing more is presently known about Wollweber.

8. BB Mus. Ms. P1082, p. 1: Toccata in G minor, BWV 915, hand of J. G. Preller. Numerous fingerings.

9. BB Mus. Ms. 1108, p. 28: Organ chorale "Liebster Jesu, wir sind hier," BWV 731, hand of J. A. Dröbs (1784—1825). Numerous fingerings. Dröbs was a pupil of J. C. Kittel, one of Bach's last students; this manuscript may stem from an earlier one by Kittel.

---

[51]Hans-Joachim Schulze ("Wie entstand die Bach-Sammlung Mempell-Preller?" *Bach-Jahrbuch 1974*, p. 119) suggests that Preller may have been a student of J. T. Krebs.

10. Leipzig, MB Ms. 7, p. 86: Fugue in E minor ("Cathedral"), BWV 533, 2, hand of J. G. Preller. Seven fingerings:

11. Leipzig, MB Ms. 7, p. 129: Organ chorale "Vom Himmel hoch," BWV 738, hand of J. G. Preller. One scale passage bears fingerings:

12. BB Mus. Ms. P281, p. 3: Toccata in D minor, BWV 913, hand of Johann Christoph Georg Bach (1747—1814). One scale passage has six fingerings. J. C. G. Bach's musical relationship to J. S. Bach is unknown.

13. BB Mus. Ms. P801, p. 57: Organ chorale "Gott, durch deine Güte" (Orgelbüchlein), BWV 600, hand of Johann Tobias Krebs. Two fingerings. Krebs (1690—1762), father of Bach's later illustrious pupil Johann Ludwig Krebs, was one of Bach's earliest pupils, studying with both J. G. Walther and Bach during the years ca. 1710—17.

14. BB Mus. Ms. P801, pp. 82—83: Organ chorale "Vom Himmel hoch," BWV Anh. 65, hand of J. T. Krebs. Few fingerings:

15. BB Mus. Ms. P801, p. 86: Organ chorale "Herr Christ, der ein'ge Gottes Sohn," BWV Anh. 77, versg. 2, hand of J. T. Krebs. Few fingerings:

16. BB Mus. Ms. P801, p. 125: Prelude and Fugue in A minor, BWV 894, hand of J. T. Krebs. Few fingerings (see p. 65 above).

17. BB Mus. Ms. P801, p. 171: Fugue on a Theme of Albinoni, BWV 951, hand of J. G. Walther. Fingerings for one left-hand descending scale passage (see p. 22 above). Walther (1684—1748) was a colleague of Bach at Weimar, where he was town organist from 1707 until his death.

18. BB Mus. Ms. P803, pp. 96—97: Fantasia in A minor, BWV 922, hand of J. T. Krebs. Few fingerings:

19. BB Mus. Ms. P803, pp. 132 & 141: Fugue in A minor, BWV 543, unknown hand from the second half of the 18th century. Few fingerings.

20. BB Mus. Ms. P804, pp. 2—3: Fugue in C minor, BWV 961, unknown hand from the first half of the 18th century. Bears a number of fingerings that are much lighter in appearance than the music (perhaps they are in pencil) and were probably added to the manuscript at some later date.

21. BB Mus. Ms. P804, p. 394: Fugue in E minor ("Cathedral"), BWV 533, 2, in the hand of a scribe from J. P. Kellner's circle. Two measures of fingering show both an original set of numbers and a second set (underneath), introduced perhaps as a later "improvement" over the original.

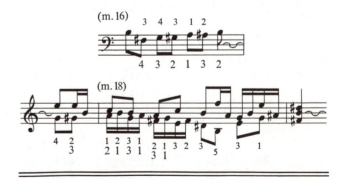

22. English Suite No. 3, BWV 808: "Allemande." *Neue Bach Ausgabe*, Series 5, Vol. 7, p. 45. Few fingerings. The *Kritischer Bericht* of this volume (ed. by Alfred Durr, Kassel: Bärenreiter, 1981, pp. 17—18 & 21) lists two sources for these fingerings:

a. BB Mus. Ms. P1072, in the hand of Anonymous 5 (working during Bach's lifetime, perhaps during the 1720s).

b. Halle, Universitäts- und Landesbibliothek Sachsen-Anhalt 12 C 14—17, in the hand of Heinrich Nicolaus Gerber (1702—75, a Bach pupil).

Appendix II

These two sources are reproduced here since their complete fingerings render them of considerable interest.

Canzona in D minor, BWV 588. Leipzig, Musikbibliothek Ms. 7 (Sammlung Mempell-Preller), pp. 95 ff. Hand of J. G. Preller.

Partita on "Sei gegrüsset," Variation I, BWV 768. Leipzig, Musikbibliothek Ms. 7, pp. 114—15. Hand of J. G. Preller.

Canzona ex D mol a 4

di Bach

58

Sei Gegrüsset, Jesu Gütig

BWV 768

Variatio I (a 2. Clav.)

Appendix III

FIVE CHORALES FROM THE ORGELBÜCHLEIN

These chorale settings have been fingered by this author according to the principles of fingering attributed to J. S. Bach in this volume. They are intended to serve as practical applications of the ideas set forth in this study.

Herr Christ, der ein'ge Gottes-Sohn, BWV 601
Gelobet seist du, Jesu Christ, BWV 604
Herr Gott, nun schleuss den Himmel auf, BWV 617
Christ lag in Todesbanden, BWV 625
Liebster Jesu, wir sind hier, BWV 633

Herr Christ, der ein'ge Gottes-Sohn
oder
Herr Gott, nun sei gepreiset
BWV 601

Gelobet seist du, Jesu Christ

à 2 Clav. & Ped.

BWV 604

Herr Gott, nun schleuss den Himmel auf
BWV 617

Christ lag in Todesbanden
BWV 625

Liebster Jesu, wir sind hier

distinctius

BWV 633

Bibliography

Adlung, Jakob. *Musica mechanica organoedi*. Berlin: Birnstiel, 1768.

Apel, Willi. *The History of Keyboard Music to 1700*. Bloomington and London: Indiana University Press, [1972].

Babitz, Sol. "On Using Early Keyboard Fingering," *Diapason*, February, March, and April 1969.

Bach, Carl Philipp Emanuel. *Versuch über die wahre Art das Clavier zu spielen*. Berlin: C. F. Henning, 1753. English translation: *Essay on the True Art of Playing Keyboard Instruments*. Trans. & ed. William J. Mitchell. New York: W. W. Norton, [1949].

Bach-Dokumente, Bde. II & III. Kassel: Bärenreiter, 1969 & 1972.

Bach, Johann Sebastian. *Clavier-büchlein vor Wilhelm Friedemann Bach*. Facsimile ed. by Ralph Kirkpatrick. New York: Da Capo, 1979.

"Bach's 'Art of Fugue': An Examination of the Sources," *Current Musicology*, No. 19. New York: Columbia University, 1975.

Boxall, Maria. *Harpsichord Method*. London: Schott, [1977].

Bruggaier, Eduard. "Studien zur Geschichte des Orgelpedalspiels in Deutschland bis zur Zeit Johann Sebastian Bachs." Unpubl. Ph. D. diss. Johann Wolfgang Goethe-Universität, Frankfurt am Main, Germany, 1959.

Burney, Charles. *The Present State of Music in Germany, the Netherlands, and United Provinces*, Vol. II. London: Backet, 1773.

——. *Carl Burney's...Tagebuch seiner Musikalischen Reisen*. Translated from the English by Johann Joachim Bode. Third volume. Hamburg: Bode, 1773.

Czerny, Carl. *Erinnerungen aus meinem Leben*, ms. 1842. Edited and annotated by W. Kolneder. Strasbourg & Baden-Baden: Heitz, 1968.

David, Hans T., and Arthur Mendel, eds. *The Bach Reader*. New York: W. W. Norton, 1966.

Dolmetsch, Arnold. *The Interpretation of Music of the Seventeenth and Eighteenth Centuries*. London: Novello, 1915; corrected edition, 1946.

Donington, Robert. *The Interpretation of Early Music*. London: Faber & Faber, [1963].

Ferguson, Howard. *Keyboard Interpretation*. New York & London: Oxford University Press, 1975.

Forkel, Johann Nicolaus. *Über Johann Sebastian Bachs Leben, Kunst und Kunstwerke*. Leipzig, 1802.

Handschriften der Werke Johann Sebastian Bachs in der Musikbibliothek der Stadt

Leipzig. Bibliographische Veröffentlichungen der Musikbibliothek der Stadt Leipzig, 1964.

Houle, George L. "The Musical Measure as Discussed by Theorists from 1650—1800." Unpubl. Ph.D. diss. Stanford University, 1961.

Humanus, P. C. *Dess musici Theoretico-Practici*. 1749.

Hummel, Johann Nepomuk. *Anweisung zum Piano-Forte-Spiel*. Vienna: Tobias Haslinger, [preface 1827].

Kirnberger, Johann Philipp. *Clavierübungen mit der Bachischen Applicatur*. 4 Sammlungen. Berlin: Friedrich Wilhelm Birnstiel, 1761, 1762, 1763, & 1766.

———. *Die Kunst des reinen Satzes in der Musik*. Vol. II, Part I, 1776. Trans. David Beach & Jurgen Thym, *The Art of Strict Musical Composition*. New Haven: Yale University Press, [1982].

Kittel, Johann Christian. *Vierstimmige Choräle mit Vorspielen*. Altona: J. F. Hammerich, 1803.

Knecht, Justin Heinrich. *Vollständige Orgelschule für Anfänger und Geübtere*. Leipzig: Breitkopf & Hartel, 1795—96.

LeHuray, Peter. "On Using Early Keyboard fingering," *Diapason*, February, March, and April 1969.

Lindley, Mark, and Maria Boxall, *Early Keyboard Fingerings: an Anthology*. London: Schott, [1982].

Liszt, Franz. *Sämtliche Orgelwerke*. Ed. Margittay. Budapest: Editio Musica, [1970].

Löffler, Hans. "Die Schüler Joh. Seb. Bachs," *Bach-Jahrbuch*, 1953, pp. 5—28.

MacClintock, Carol, ed. *Readings in the History of Music in Performance*. Bloomington & London: Indiana University Press, [c. 1979].

Marpurg, Friedrich Wilhelm. *Anleitung zum Clavierspielen*. Second ed. Berlin: Haude und Spener, 1765.

Mattheson, Johann. *Kleine general-bass-schule*. Hamburg, 1735.

Mozart, J. G. Leopold. *Versuch einer gründlichen Violinschule*. Augsburg: J. J. Lotter, 1756.

Muffat, Gottlieb. *Componimenti Musicali*. [Ca. 1739.]

Müller, August Eberhard. *Forte-piano-Schule*. Leipzig: C. P. Peters, [1804].

Petri, Samuel. *Anleitung zur praktischen Musik*. Lauban: J. C. Wirthgen, 1767 & 1782.

Quantz, Johann Joachim. *Versuch einer Anweisung die Flöte traversiere zu spielen*. Berlin: J. F. Voss, 1752.

Rameau, Jean-Philippe. *Pieces de Clavessin*. Paris, 1724.

Rellstab, Johann Carl Friedrich. *C. P. E. Bachs Anfangsstücke mit einer Anleitung den Gebrauch dieser Stücke die Bachsche Fingersetzung, die Manieren und den Vortrag betreffend*. Berlin: Verlage der Rellstabschen Musikhandlung...1789.

Rodgers, Julane. "Early Keyboard Fingering, ca. 1520—1620." Unpubl. D. M. A. diss. University of Oregon, 1971.

Schneider, Friedrich. *Handbuch des Organisten*. Halberstadt: Carl Brüggemann, 1830.

Schulze, Hans-Joachim. " 'Das Stück in Goldpapier': Ermittlungen zu einigen Bach-Abschriften des frühen 18. Jahrhunderts," *Bach-Jahrbuch*, 1978, pp. 19—42.

———. "Wie entstand die Bach-Sammlung Mempell-Preller?" *Bach-Jahrbuch*, 1974, pp. 104—20.

Schwendowius, Barbara, and Wolfgang Dömling, eds. *Johann Sebastian Bach: Life/Times/Influence*. Kassel: Bärenreiter, [1977].

Soderlund, Sandra, *Organ Technique: An Historical Approach*. Chapel Hill, N. C.: Hinshaw, 1980.

Spitta, Philipp. *Johann Sebastian Bach*. English translation, London, 1889. Reprinted, New York: Dover, 1951.

Türk, Daniel Gottlob. *Klavierschule*. Leipzig und Halle: Schwickert, 1789.

———. *Kleines Lehrbuch für Anfänger im Klavierspielen*. Halle u. Leipzig: Schwickert, 1802.

———. *Von den wichtigsten Pflichten eines Organisten*. Halle: Schwickert, 1787.

Wegweiser, by Johann Speth (?). Augsburg, 1689.

Williams, Peter. *The Organ Music of J. S. Bach*, Vol. I. Cambridge: Cambridge University Press, [1980].

Zavarsky, Ernest. "Zum Pedalspiel des jungen Johann Sebastian Bach," *Musikforschung*, Vol. 18 (1965), pp. 370—78.

Zehnder, Jean-Claude. "Alte Fingersätze," *Ars Organi*, September 1980, pp. 16 ff.

———. "Organ Articulation in the Seventeenth and Eighteenth Centuries," *The American Organist*; Part I, Vol. 17, No. 7 (July 1983); Part II, Vol. 17, No. 12 (December 1983); revised reprint of "Zur Artikulation im Orgelspiel des 17. und 18. Jahrhunderts," *Musik und Gottesdienst*, Vols. 2 & 3, 1977.